SELF SERVICE REPORTING USING POWER BI WITHIN DYNAMICS AX 2012

Murray Fife

ISBN-13: 978-1541250550

ISBN-10: 1541250559

Preface

What You Need for this Guide

All the examples shown in this blueprint were done with the Microsoft Dynamics AX 2012 virtual machine image that was downloaded from the Microsoft CustomerSource or PartnerSource site. If you don't have your own installation of Microsoft Dynamics AX 2012, you can also use the images found on the Microsoft Learning Download Center or deployed through Lifecycle Services. The following list of software from the virtual image was leveraged within this guide:

Microsoft Dynamics AX 2012 R3 CU9 or higher

Even though all the preceding software was used during the development and testing of the recipes in this book, they may also work on earlier versions of the software with minor tweaks and adjustments, and should also work on later versions without any changes.

Errata

Although we have taken every care to ensure the accuracy of our content, mistakes do happen. If you find a mistake in one of our books—maybe a mistake in the text or the code—we would be grateful if you would report this to us. By doing so, you can save other readers from frustration and help us improve subsequent versions of this book. If you find any errata, please report them by emailing editor@dynamicsaxcompanions.com.

Piracy

Piracy of copyright material on the Internet is an ongoing problem across all media. If you come across any illegal copies of our works, in any form, on the Internet, please provide us with the location address or website name immediately so that we can pursue a remedy.

Please contact us at legal@dynamicsaxcompanions.com with a link to the suspected pirated material.

We appreciate your help in protecting our authors, and our ability to bring you valuable content.

Questions

You can contact us at help@dynamicsaxcompanions.com if you are having a problem with any aspect of the book, and we will do our best to address it.

 www.dynamicscompanions.com
Dynamics Companions

- 1 -

www.blindsquirrelpublishing.com
© 2016 Blind Squirrel Publishing, LLC , All Rights Reserved

BLIND SQUIRREL
PUBLISHING

dync
dynamics companions

www.dynamicscompanions.com
Dynamics Companions

www.blindsquirrelpublishing.com
© 2016 Blind Squirrel Publishing, LLC, All Rights Reserved

BLIND SQUIRREL
PUBLISHING

Table of Contents

Introduction

Maybe you thought that the only thing that is better than Power BI within Excel is Power BI Online, but you are so wrong was wrong. The Power BI Desktop application that is available from the Power BI website is much better and everyone needs to use it.

The Power BI Desktop is a standalone dashboard designing tool that takes all of the great features within Excel like Power Query, PowerView, and PowerPivot and puts them in one single place to make all of your reporting a synch. And after you have finished building your dashboards, you can then publish them to the new hosted Power BI portal and create your own custom dashboards, and even perform Q&A on the data just by typing in the questions that you want answered.

In this guide we will look at this new tool and how you can use it to quickly analyze all of your Dynamics AX data and also blend in multiple data feeds into one dashboard to view all of the data that you need all in one place.

Topics Covered

- Signing up for the free version of Power BI Online
- Using the preconfigured dashboard packages
- Downloading the Power BI desktop application
- Getting your reporting data into Power BI
- Using the Report View to create dashboards
- Accessing the Query Editor
- Changing data's Data Types through the Query Editor
- Accessing the Data Editor
- Using the Data Editor to change data types
- Saving the Dashboard Projects
- Renaming fields to make them more friendly to the user
- Viewing the changes in Query Editor
- Create more detailed dashboards
- Publishing Dashboards to Power BI on Office365
- Creating a new dashboard in Power BI Online
- Pinning Report Tiles to your Dashboards
- Using Q&A to build dashboards just by asking for the data
- Using the Field Explorer to help find data
- Downloading the Power BI Mobile App
- Connecting the Power BI Mobile App to Power BI Online

Signing up for the free version of Power BI Online

You don't have to invest a lot of money in order to try out Power BI, in fact you don't have to spend any money at all. You can sign up for the personal version for **free**

How to do it...

When you log into your Power BI site (www.Power BI.com), you will see that there is an option to **Use It Free**.

If you don't believe it, just type in yourO365 email account and click the button.

Power BI will then start hydrating your very own Power BI workspace...

And within a couple of second you will have your own blank Power BI workspace.

www.dynamicscompanions.com
Dynamics Companions

- 5 -

Signing up for the free version of Power BI Online

How to do it...

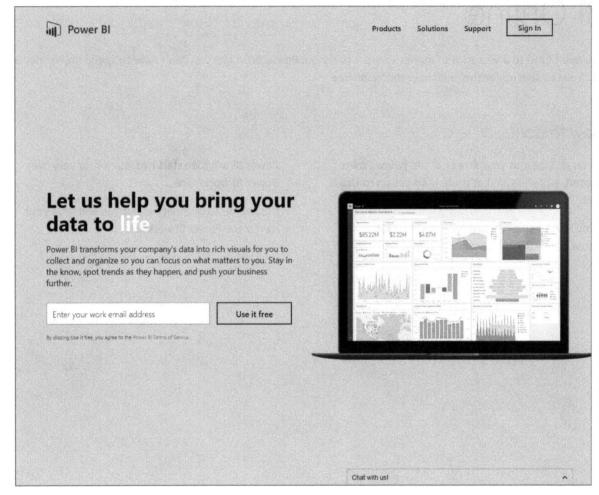

When you log into your Power BI site (www.Power BI.com), you will see that there is an option to **Use It Free**.

www.dynamicscompanions.com
Dynamics Companions

- 6 -

www.blindsquirrelpublishing.com
© 2016 Blind Squirrel Publishing, LLC, All Rights Reserved

BLIND SQUIRREL
PUBLISHING

Signing up for the free version of Power BI Online

How to do it...

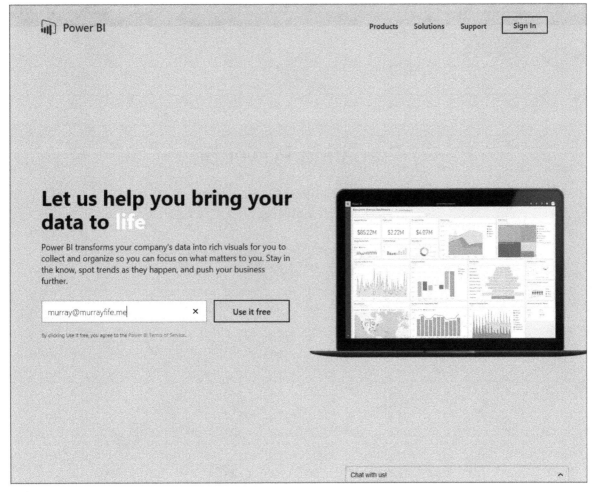

If you don't believe it, just type in yourO365 email account and click the button.

Signing up for the free version of Power BI Online

How to do it...

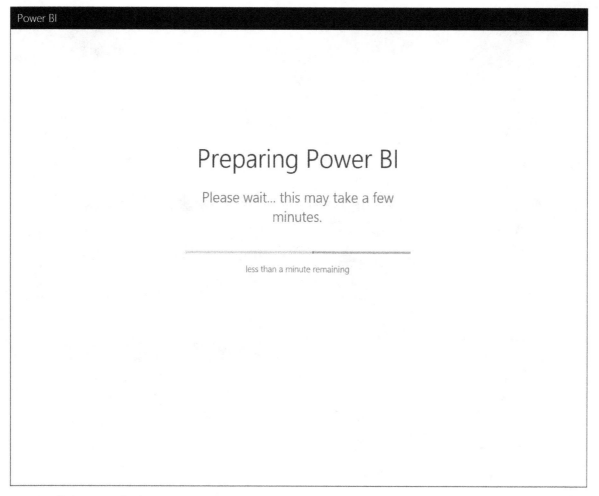

Power BI will then start hydrating your very own Power BI workspace...

Signing up for the free version of Power BI Online

How to do it...

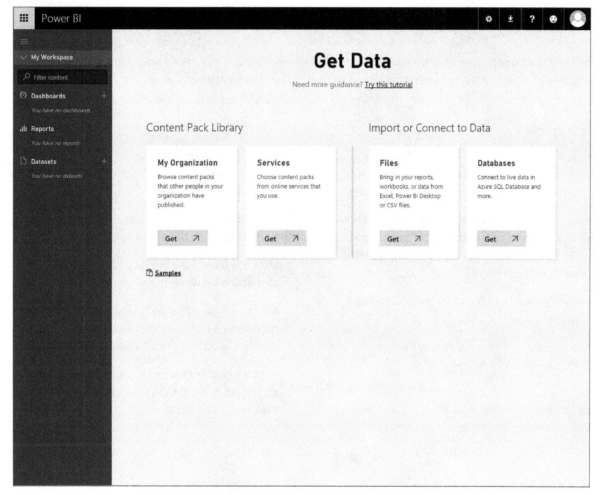

And within a couple of second you will have your own blank Power BI workspace.

www.dynamicscompanions.com
Dynamics Companions

- 9 -

www.blindsquirrelpublishing.com
© 2016 Blind Squirrel Publishing, LLC , All Rights Reserved

BLIND SQUIRREL
PUBLISHING

Using the preconfigured dashboard packages

Before we start creating our own dashboards and reports from our data, let's take a quick look at the Pre-configured packages that come with Power BI – you may not have to do any work at all...

How to do it...

On the welcome screen for Power BI there are a number of different places that you can get data from. The **Services** is one of the most interesting.

Within the **Services** data service you'll find a whole slew of different pre-configured dashboards that can be linked to different services. All they need is the connection information.

For example, we can connect to your own Google Analytics account.

When you start the connection it will ask you for the connection information.

Here's the secret decoder ring for this option – the **Account, Property**, and **View** are just the three levels within your Google Analytics connection.

All you have to do is type in the connection information (this is case sensitive) and click on the **Next** button.

Then you will be asked to sign in with your credentials using the oAuth2 protocol.

After you have done that you just authorize the connection between the services.

After you have done that you will be taken to a pre-configured dashboard for that service and Power BI will start hydrating the dashboards with your data.

Within a couple of seconds you will have a fully loaded analytics Dashboard and you didn't even have to break a sweat.

Using the preconfigured dashboard packages

How to do it...

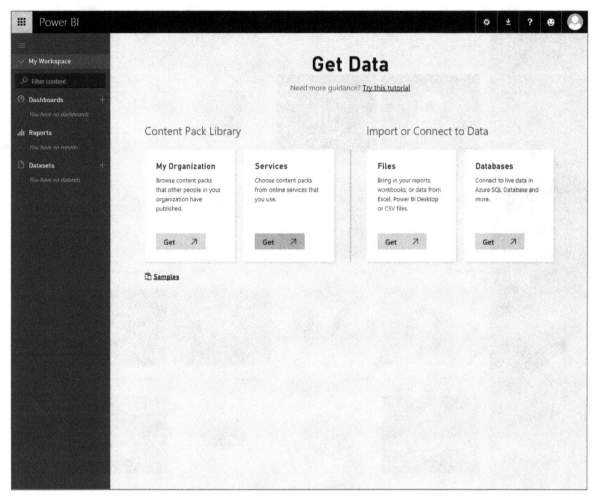

On the welcome screen for Power BI there are a number of different places that you can get data from. The **Services** is one of the most interesting.

www.dynamicscompanions.com
Dynamics Companions
- 11 -
www.blindsquirrelpublishing.com
© 2016 Blind Squirrel Publishing, LLC , All Rights Reserved
BLIND SQUIRREL
PUBLISHING

Using the preconfigured dashboard packages

How to do it...

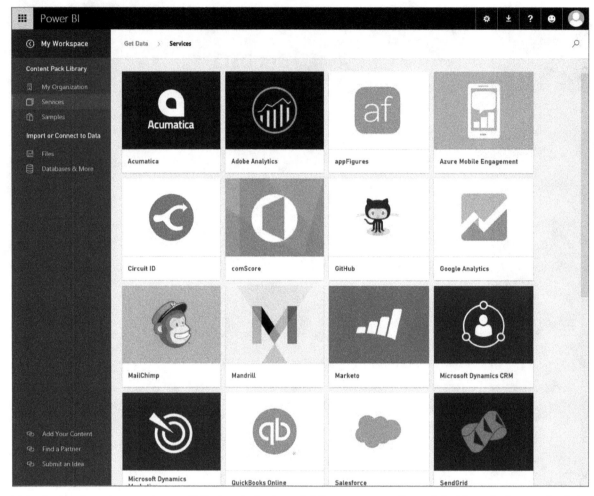

Within the **Services** data service you'll find a whole slew of different pre-configured dashboards that can be linked to different services. All they need is the connection information.

Using the preconfigured dashboard packages

How to do it...

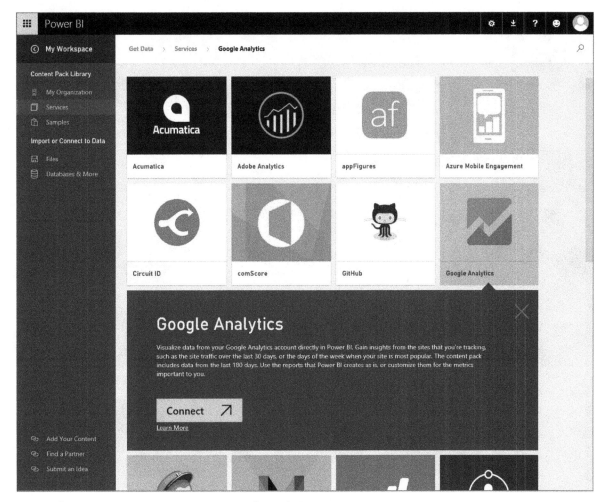

For example, we can connect to your own Google Analytics account.

www.dynamicscompanions.com
Dynamics Companions

- 13 -

www.blindsquirrelpublishing.com
© 2016 Blind Squirrel Publishing, LLC , All Rights Reserved

BLIND SQUIRREL
PUBLISHING

Using the preconfigured dashboard packages

How to do it...

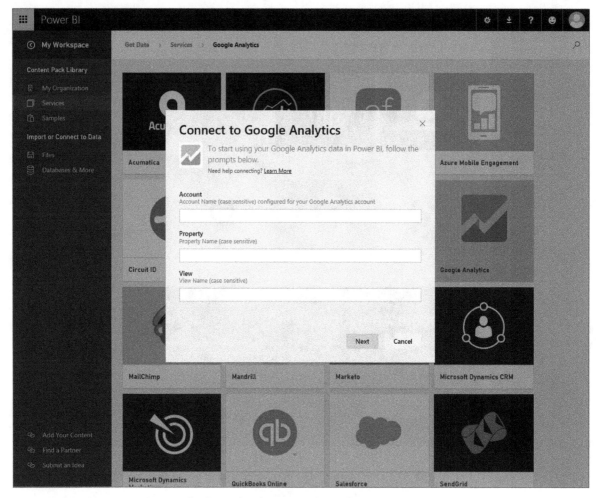

When you start the connection it will ask you for the connection information.

Using the preconfigured dashboard packages

How to do it...

Here's the secret decoder ring for this option – the **Account, Property**, and **View** are just the three levels within your Google Analytics connection.

dyn c
www.dynamicscompanions.com
Dynamics Companions

- 15 -

www.blindsquirrelpublishing.com
© 2016 Blind Squirrel Publishing, LLC , All Rights Reserved

BLIND SQUIRREL
PUBLISHING

Using the preconfigured dashboard packages

How to do it...

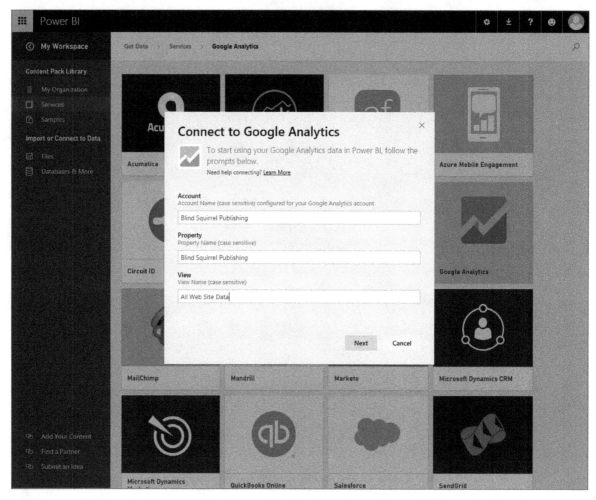

All you have to do is type in the connection information (this is case sensitive) and click on the **Next** button.

dync
www.dynamicscompanions.com
Dynamics Companions

- 16 -

www.blindsquirrelpublishing.com
© 2016 Blind Squirrel Publishing, LLC , All Rights Reserved

BLIND SQUIRREL
PUBLISHING

Using the preconfigured dashboard packages

How to do it...

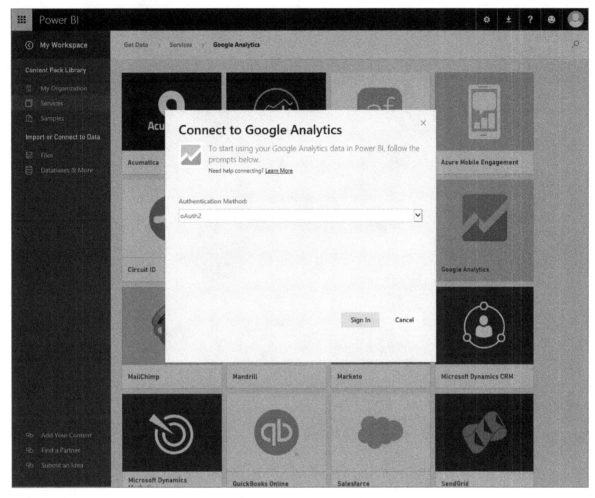

Then you will be asked to sign in with your credentials using the oAuth2 protocol.

dync
www.dynamicscompanions.com
Dynamics Companions

- 17 -

www.blindsquirrelpublishing.com
© 2016 Blind Squirrel Publishing, LLC , All Rights Reserved

BLIND SQUIRREL
PUBLISHING

Using the preconfigured dashboard packages

How to do it...

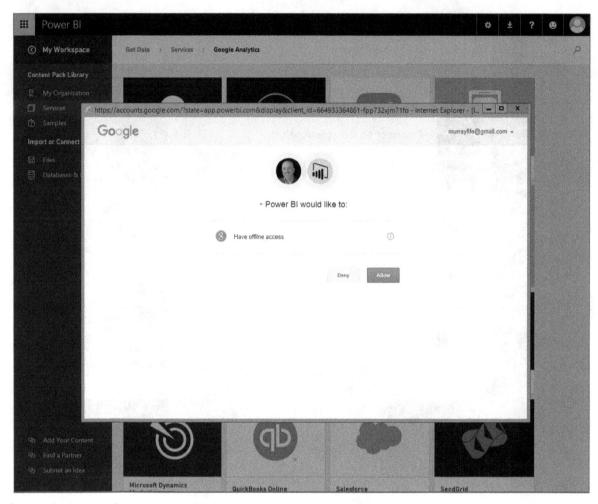

After you have done that you just authorize the connection between the services.

Using the preconfigured dashboard packages

How to do it...

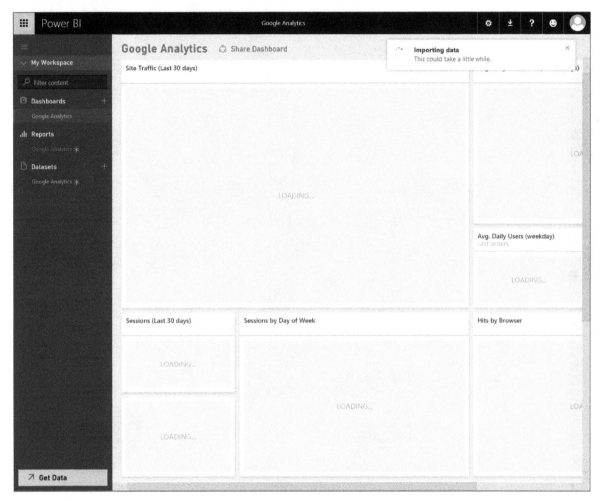

After you have done that you will be taken to a pre-configured dashboard for that service and Power BI will start hydrating the dashboards with your data.

Using the preconfigured dashboard packages

How to do it...

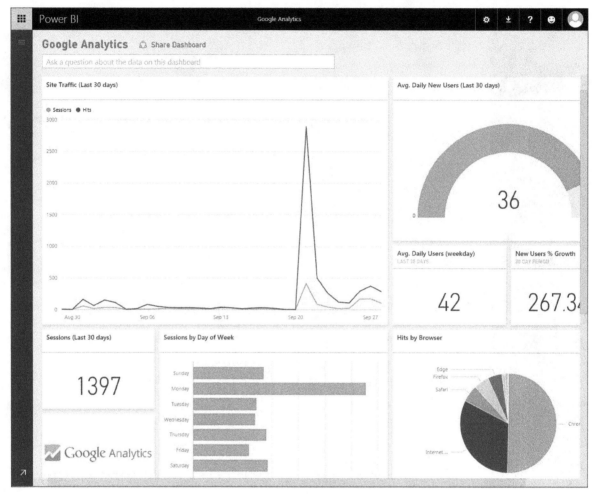

Within a couple of seconds you will have a fully loaded analytics Dashboard and you didn't even have to break a sweat.

dync

www.dynamicscompanions.com
Dynamics Companions

- 20 -

www.blindsquirrelpublishing.com
© 2016 Blind Squirrel Publishing, LLC , All Rights Reserved

BLIND SQUIRREL
PUBLISHING

Downloading the Power BI desktop application

Although you can get data directly from within Power BI Online and generate your dashboards, there is a much easier way to create your dashboards on your desktop using the Power BI Desktop Application. And it's free to download as well.

How to do it...

To get your copy, just click on the dropdown icon in the top right of the **Power BI Online** website and you will see an option to get the **Power BI Desktop**

If you click on it then you will be able to download the install files.

Alternatively you can go to **Power BI.com** site and click on the **Power BI Desktop** link within the **Products** dropdown menu.

That will take you to the product page and you will be able to download the install files from there as well.

All you have to do is click through the welcome page...

Accept the obligatory license agreement...

Tell it where to install...

And click **Install**.

After it is done, click on the **Finish** button and you are done.

The next thing that you know the Power BI Desktop application will be waiting for you to start plundering some data.

www.dynamicscompanions.com
Dynamics Companions

- 21 -

www.blindsquirrelpublishing.com
© 2016 Blind Squirrel Publishing, LLC , All Rights Reserved

BLIND SQUIRREL
PUBLISHING

Downloading the Power BI desktop application

How to do it...

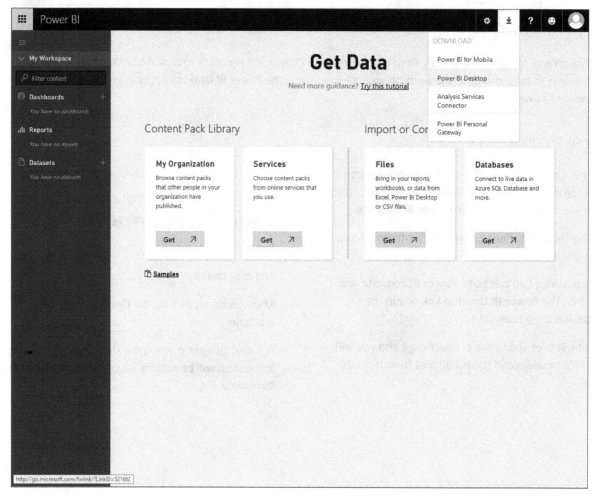

To get your copy, just click on the dropdown icon in the top right of the **Power BI Online** website and you will see an option to get the **Power BI Desktop**

Downloading the Power BI desktop application

How to do it...

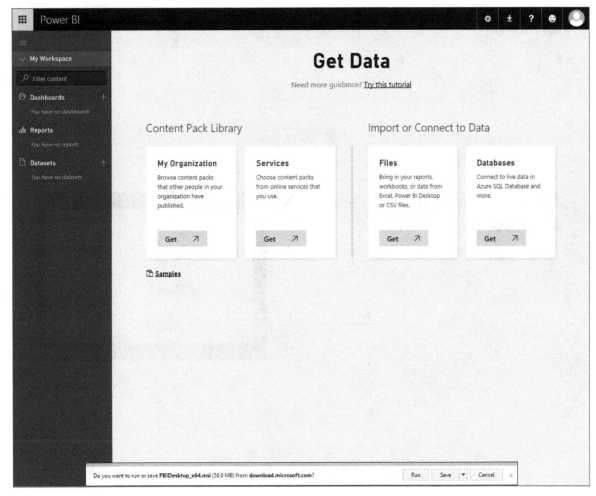

If you click on it then you will be able to download the install files.

www.dynamicscompanions.com
Dynamics Companions

- 23 -

www.blindsquirrelpublishing.com
© 2016 Blind Squirrel Publishing, LLC, All Rights Reserved

BLIND SQUIRREL
PUBLISHING

Downloading the Power BI desktop application

How to do it...

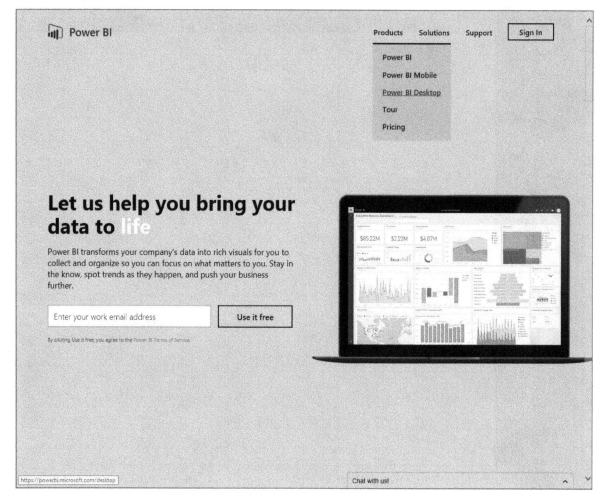

Alternatively you can go to **Power BI.com** site and click on the **Power BI Desktop** link within the **Products** dropdown menu.

Downloading the Power BI desktop application

How to do it...

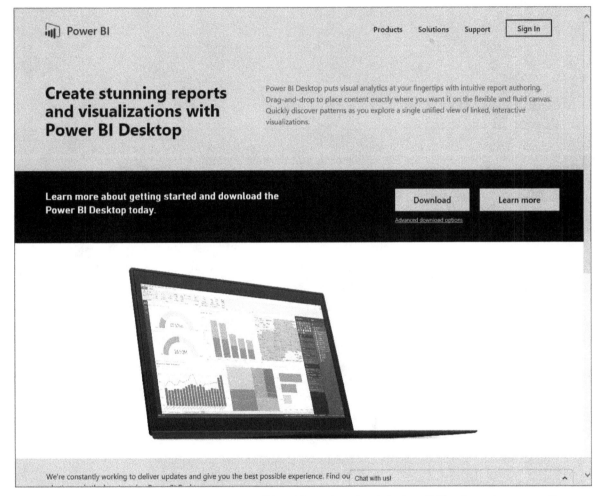

That will take you to the product page and you will be able to download the install files from there as well.

Downloading the Power BI desktop application

How to do it...

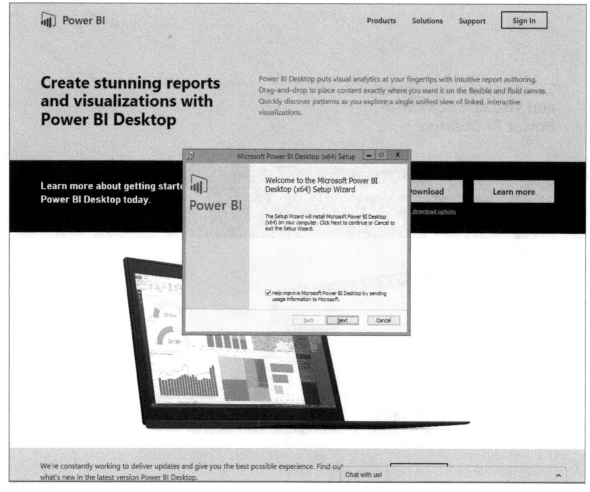

All you have to do is click through the welcome page...

Downloading the Power BI desktop application

How to do it...

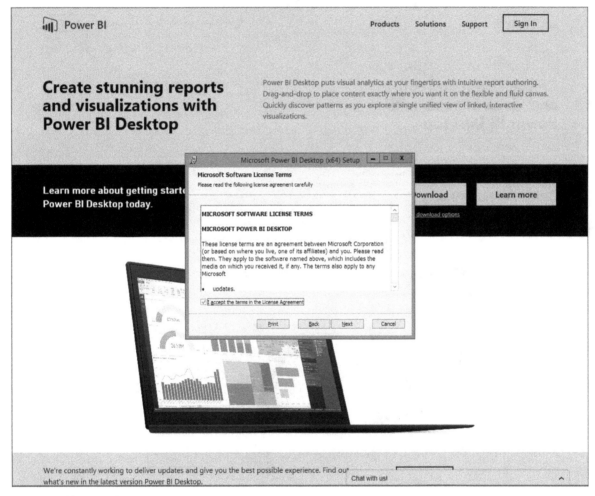

Accept the obligatory license agreement...

www.dynamicscompanions.com
Dynamics Companions

- 27 -

www.blindsquirrelpublishing.com
© 2016 Blind Squirrel Publishing, LLC , All Rights Reserved

BLIND SQUIRREL
PUBLISHING

Downloading the Power BI desktop application

How to do it...

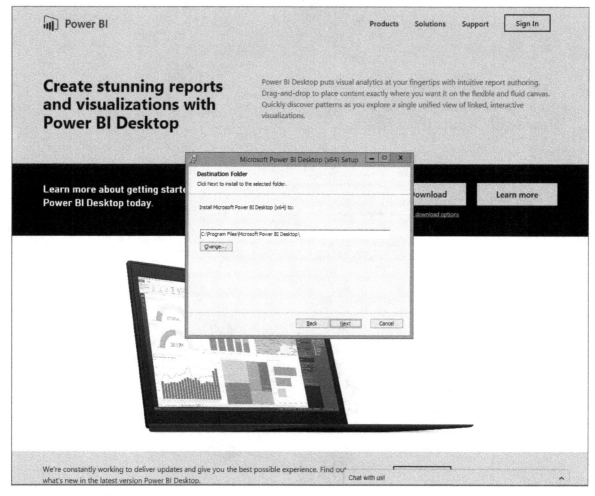

Tell it where to install...

Downloading the Power BI desktop application

How to do it...

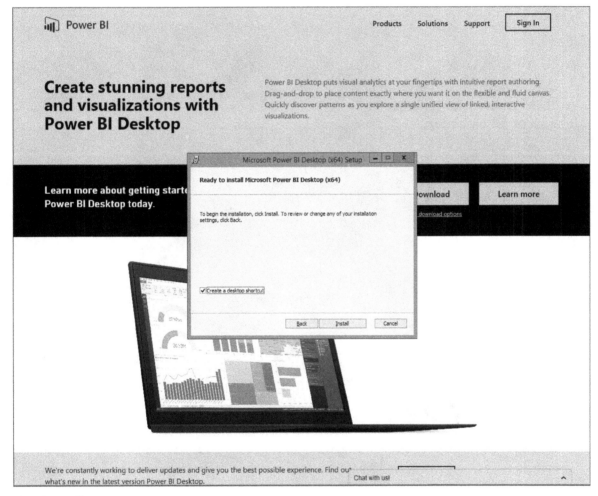

And click **Install**.

Downloading the Power BI desktop application

How to do it...

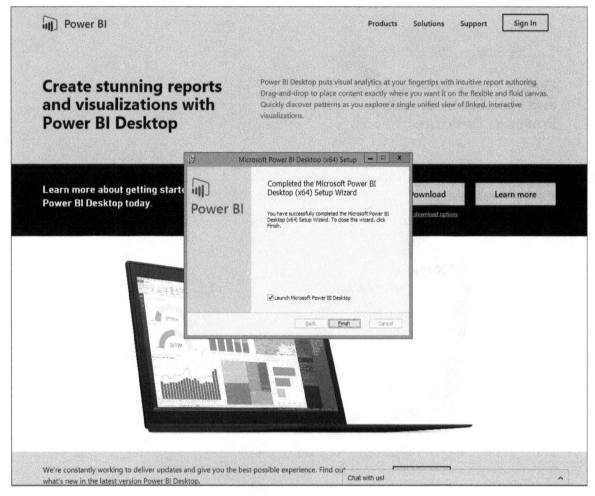

After it is done, click on the **Finish** button and you are done.

Downloading the Power BI desktop application

How to do it...

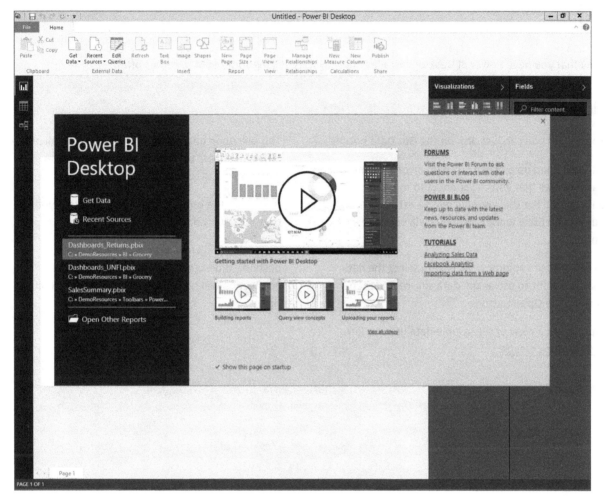

The next thing that you know the Power BI Desktop application will be waiting for you to start plundering some data.

www.dynamicscompanions.com
Dynamics Companions

- 31 -

www.blindsquirrelpublishing.com
© 2016 Blind Squirrel Publishing, LLC, All Rights Reserved

BLIND SQUIRREL
PUBLISHING

Getting your reporting data into Power BI

Now that you have Power BI Desktop installed you can start getting some data to report off.

How to do it...

To start off you can just click on the **Get Data** option.

This will open up a dialog box with all of the different data sources that you can connect to for your dashboard. For this example, we've extracted data out into an Excel workbook so we will use the **Excel** option.

When the file explorer is displayed, select the data that you want to use as the data source and then click on the **Open** button.

Tip: To get a copy of the sample data use this link: https://doc.co/sjuSP1

This will open up a Navigator showing you all of the different sheets that are available within the workbook.

Just select the one with all of the data that you want to report off and click on the **Load** button.

Next thing you know you will be taken to a dashboard designer workspace and your data connection will be shown in the fields panel on the right.

Getting your reporting data into Power BI

How to do it...

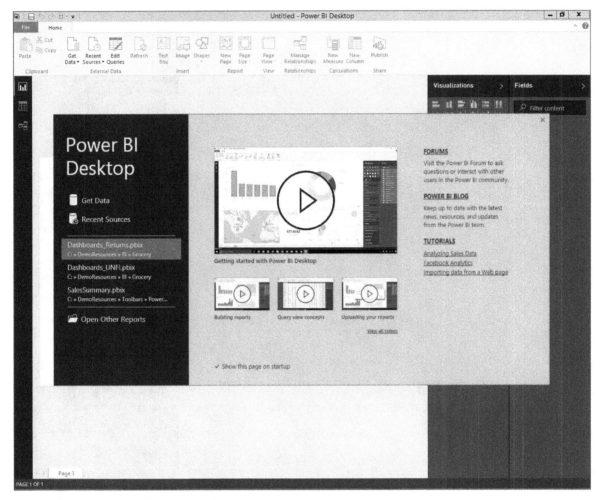

To start off you can just click on the **Get Data** option.

www.dynamicscompanions.com
Dynamics Companions

- 33 -

www.blindsquirrelpublishing.com
© 2016 Blind Squirrel Publishing, LLC , All Rights Reserved

BLIND SQUIRREL
PUBLISHING

Getting your reporting data into Power BI

How to do it...

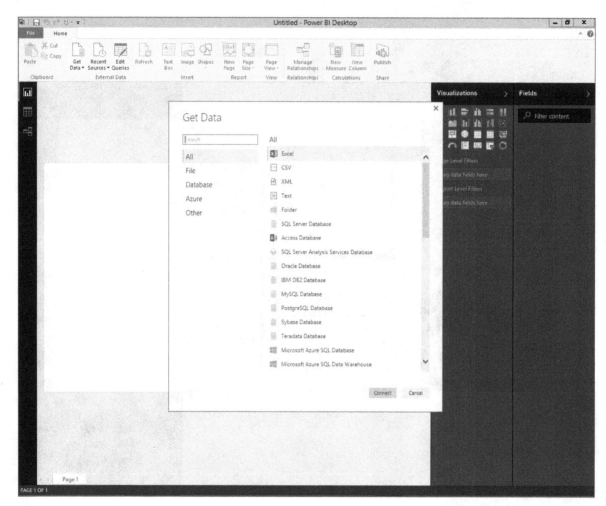

This will open up a dialog box with all of the different data sources that you can connect to for your dashboard. For this example, we've extracted data out into an Excel workbook so we will use the **Excel** option.

Getting your reporting data into Power BI

How to do it...

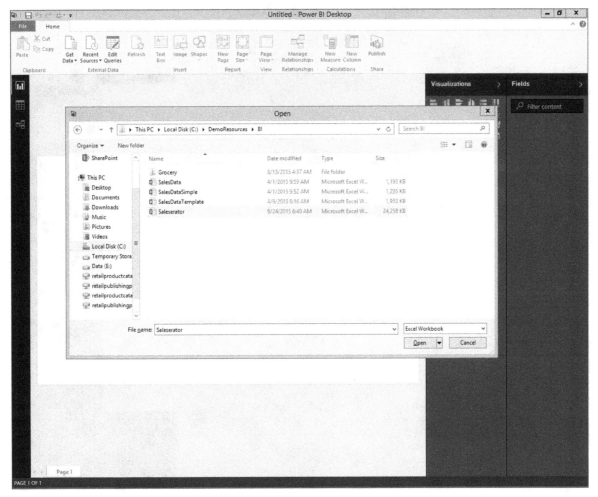

When the file explorer is displayed, select the data that you want to use as the data source and then click on the **Open** button.

Tip: To get a copy of the sample data use this link: https://doc.co/sjuSP1

www.dynamicscompanions.com
Dynamics Companions
- 35 -
www.blindsquirrelpublishing.com
© 2016 Blind Squirrel Publishing, LLC, All Rights Reserved
BLIND SQUIRREL
PUBLISHING

Getting your reporting data into Power BI

How to do it...

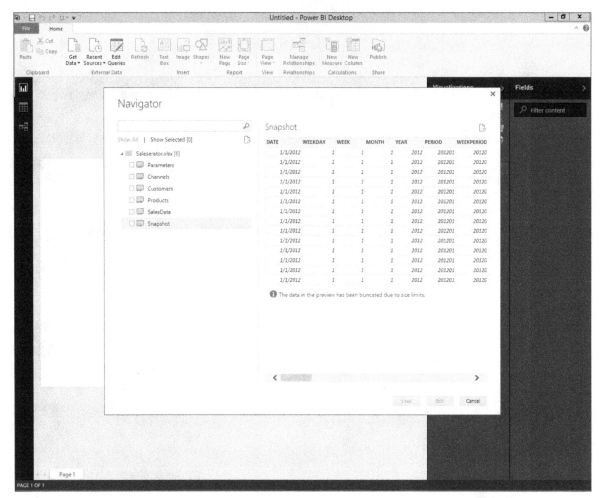

This will open up a Navigator showing you all of the different sheets that are available within the workbook.

Getting your reporting data into Power BI

How to do it...

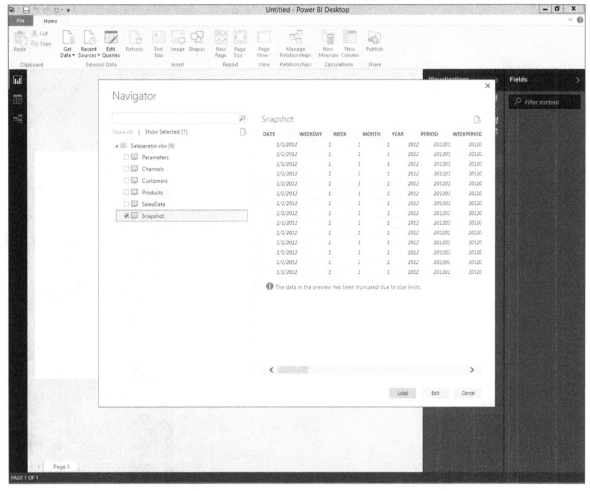

Just select the one with all of the data that you want to report off and click on the **Load** button.

www.dynamicscompanions.com
Dynamics Companions

- 37 -

www.blindsquirrelpublishing.com
© 2016 Blind Squirrel Publishing, LLC , All Rights Reserved

BLIND SQUIRREL
PUBLISHING

Getting your reporting data into Power BI

How to do it...

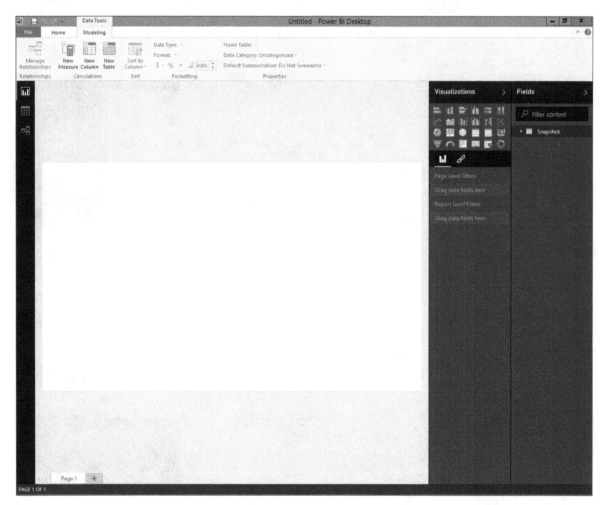

Next thing you know you will be taken to a dashboard designer workspace and your data connection will be shown in the fields panel on the right.

www.dynamicscompanions.com
Dynamics Companions

- 38 -

www.blindsquirrelpublishing.com
© 2016 Blind Squirrel Publishing, LLC , All Rights Reserved

BLIND SQUIRREL
PUBLISHING

Using the Report View to create dashboards

Now that you have the data loaded you might as well start creating some dashboards with it.

How to do it...

If you expand out the fields within the Field panel you will see all of the columns from the worksheet are available for you to report off.

Now we can start building our dashboard. We will start off by selecting the **STATE** field and it will be added directly to the canvas.

Next we can add a measure to the report, so click on the **TOTAL** field from the field chooser.

If you want to resize the table then you can just grab the edges of the table and drag them out to the boundaries of the canvas.

You will notice in the **Visualizations** panel there are a lot of different ways that we can look at the data.

If you click on the icon that looks like a globe, then the report will change to show you all of the sales by state as a map.

You can also change the visualization of the totals for each of the states now by adding a measure field to the **Color Saturation** field. To do this just drag the **TOTAL** field over to the **Color Saturation** field in the **Visualizations** panel.

As an alternative way to vies the mapped data, click on the icon in the visualization that looks like a checkerboard map. This will change the view from dots for each of the states to colored sections.

Using the Report View to create dashboards

How to do it...

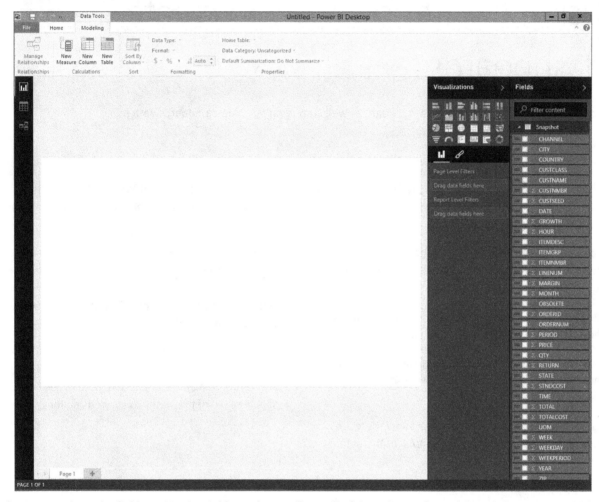

If you expand out the fields within the Field panel you will see all of the columns from the worksheet are available for you to report off.

dyn c

www.dynamicscompanions.com
Dynamics Companions

- 40 -

www.blindsquirrelpublishing.com
© 2016 Blind Squirrel Publishing, LLC , All Rights Reserved

BLIND SQUIRREL
PUBLISHING

Using the Report View to create dashboards

How to do it...

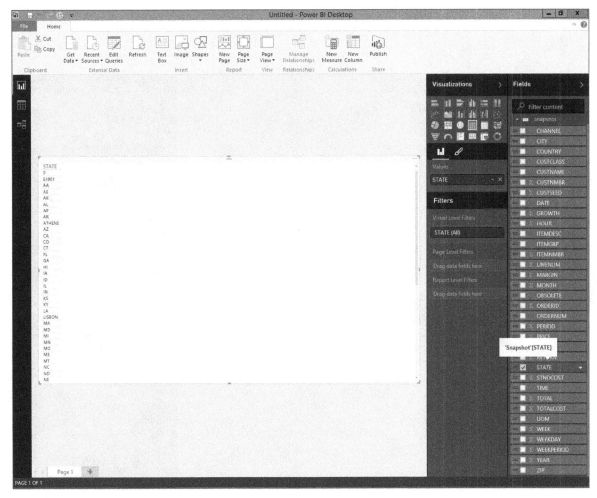

Now we can start building our dashboard. We will start off by selecting the **STATE** field and it will be added directly to the canvas.

Using the Report View to create dashboards

How to do it...

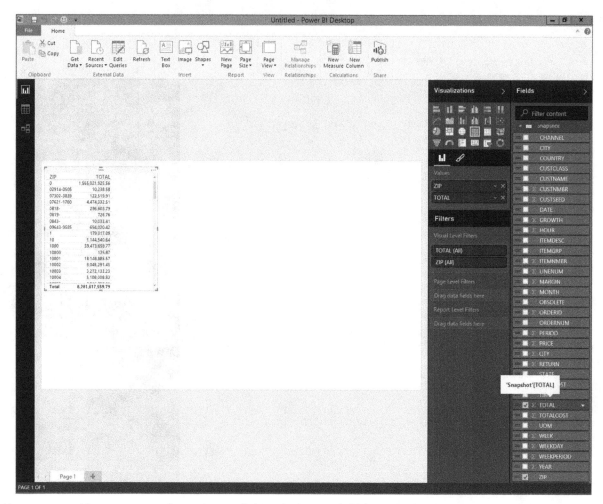

Next we can add a measure to the report, so click on the **TOTAL** field from the field chooser.

www.dynamicscompanions.com
Dynamics Companions

- 42 -

www.blindsquirrelpublishing.com
© 2016 Blind Squirrel Publishing, LLC , All Rights Reserved

BLIND SQUIRREL
PUBLISHING

Using the Report View to create dashboards

How to do it...

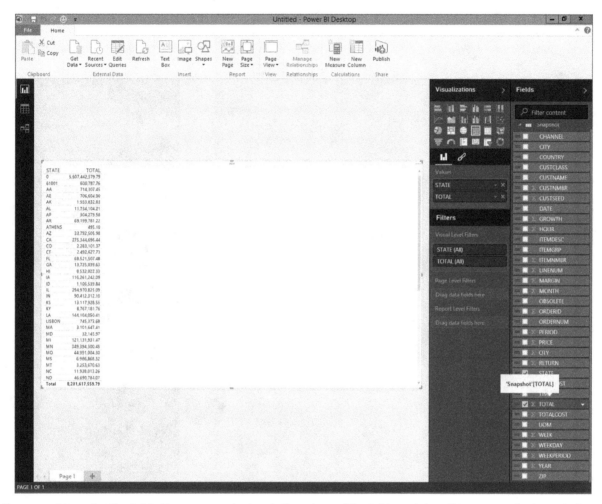

If you want to resize the table then you can just grab the edges of the table and drag them out to the boundaries of the canvas.

Using the Report View to create dashboards

How to do it...

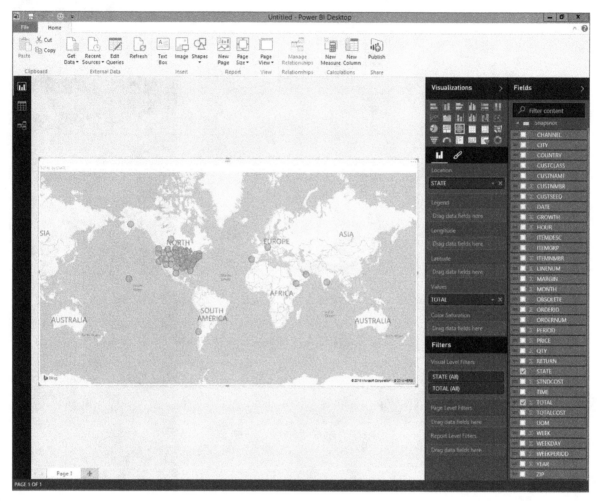

You will notice in the **Visualizations** panel there are a lot of different ways that we can look at the data. If you click on the icon that looks like a globe, then the report will change to show you all of the sales by state as a map.

www.dynamicscompanions.com
Dynamics Companions

- 44 -

www.blindsquirrelpublishing.com
© 2016 Blind Squirrel Publishing, LLC, All Rights Reserved

BLIND SQUIRREL
PUBLISHING

Using the Report View to create dashboards

How to do it...

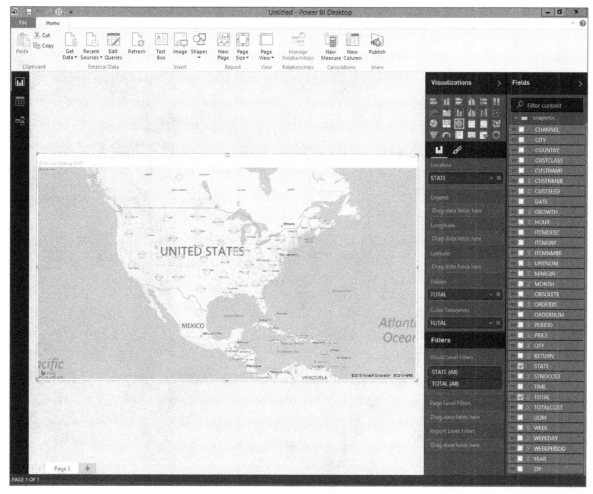

You can also change the visualization of the totals for each of the states now by adding a measure field to the **Color Saturation** field. To do this just drag the **TOTAL** field over to the **Color Saturation** field in the **Visualizations** panel.

Using the Report View to create dashboards

How to do it...

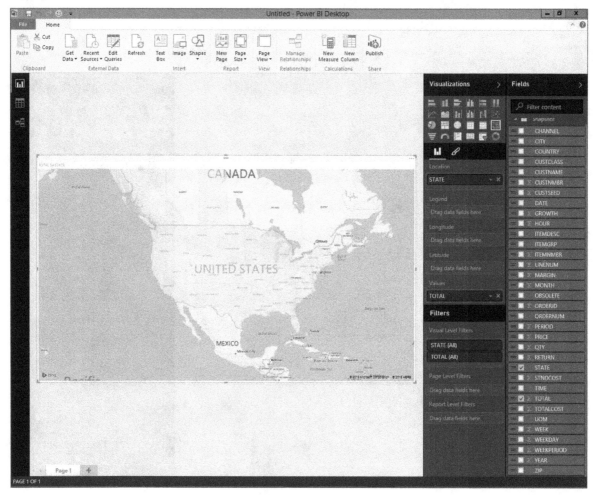

As an alternative way to vies the mapped data, click on the icon in the visualization that looks like a checkerboard map. This will change the view from dots for each of the states to colored sections.

dyn c
www.dynamicscompanions.com
Dynamics Companions

- 46 -

www.blindsquirrelpublishing.com
© 2016 Blind Squirrel Publishing, LLC, All Rights Reserved

BLIND SQUIRREL
PUBLISHING

Accessing the Query Editor

You may have noticed a couple of things that don't quite look right with the data fields that were created during the loading of the data. Some of the dimensions have been marked as measures and also the names look a little too loud since they are all in upper case.

Don't worry, Power BI has a Query Editor that allows you to tidy up the data.

How to do it...

To access the **Query Editor** just click on the **Edit Query** button within the **External Data** button group of the **Home** ribbon bar.

This will open up the **Query Editor** and you will see all of the data that you list loaded is displayed in a grid.

www.dynamicscompanions.com
Dynamics Companions

- 47 -

www.blindsquirrelpublishing.com
© 2016 Blind Squirrel Publishing, LLC , All Rights Reserved

BLIND SQUIRREL
PUBLISHING

Accessing the Query Editor

How to do it...

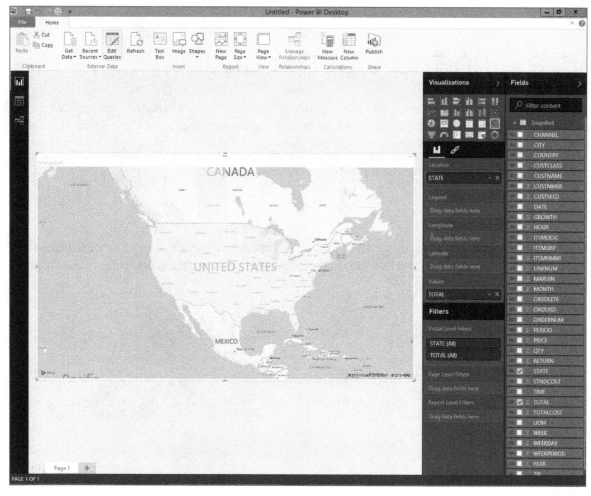

To access the **Query Editor** just click on the **Edit Query** button within the **External Data** button group of the **Home** ribbon bar.

dyn c
www.dynamicscompanions.com
Dynamics Companions
- 48 -
www.blindsquirrelpublishing.com
© 2016 Blind Squirrel Publishing, LLC , All Rights Reserved
BLIND SQUIRREL PUBLISHING

Accessing the Query Editor

How to do it...

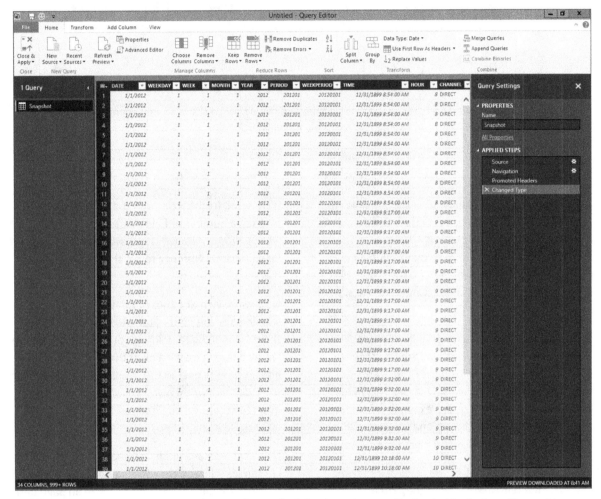

This will open up the **Query Editor** and you will see all of the data that you list loaded is displayed in a grid.

www.dynamicscompanions.com
Dynamics Companions

- 49 -

www.blindsquirrelpublishing.com
© 2016 Blind Squirrel Publishing, LLC , All Rights Reserved

BLIND SQUIRREL
PUBLISHING

Changing data's Data Types through the Query Editor

Now that we are in the **Query Editor** we can start polishing up the data. To start off, lets change the datatypes of the columns of data so that they can be charted correctly by Power BI

How to do it...

If you select any of the columns then you are able to change the datatype of the column from the default that was guessed by Power BI when it imported the data. For example, if you click on the **DATE** field then you will be able to click on the **Data Type** button in the ribbon bar and select the **Date** data type.

In this example, there are a lot of fields that are showing up as numerical fields when in fact they should be treated as text. Numerical fields are usually summed up by Power BI whereas Text fields are more dimensional. So in this example we select all of the fields that are numbers and then click on the **Data Type** dropdown list and mark them as **Text**.

Now you will notice that all of the fields are showing up as text – the telltale sign is that they are all left justified.

Next we will also select the **TIME** field and change its data type to **Time** to make it a little more concise.

If we scroll further over into the data then we will also see a number of fields that are currency based. To tidy up the data we will change their data type to **Fixed Decimal Number** to get them ready to be marked as currency.

Now we have made these updates all of the fields should have the right datatype associated with them. One thing to point out at this point is that the Query Editor is tracking all of these changes for us and if you look over in the **Applied Steps** section of the Query Editor then you will see that there is a new step there called **Changed Type** which is storing all of these changes.

Now that we have made the changes to the query we can just click on the **Close & Apply** button to save the changes and return back to the main page of the designer.

Changing data's Data Types through the Query Editor

How to do it...

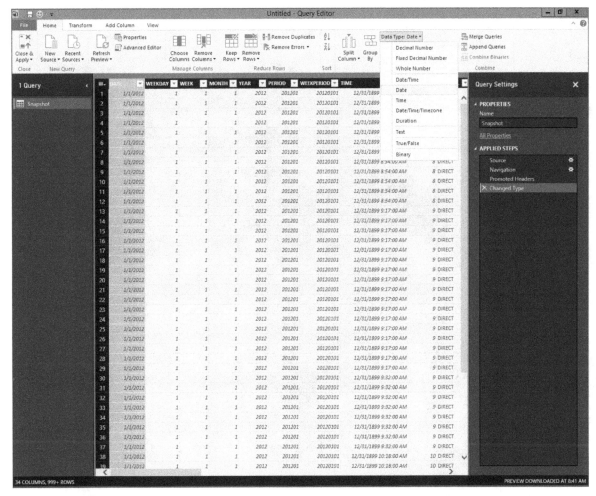

If you select any of the columns then you are able to change the datatype of the column from the default that was guessed by Power BI when it imported the data. For example, if you click on the **DATE** field then you will be able to click on the **Data Type** button in the ribbon bar and select the **Date** data type.

Changing data's Data Types through the Query Editor

How to do it...

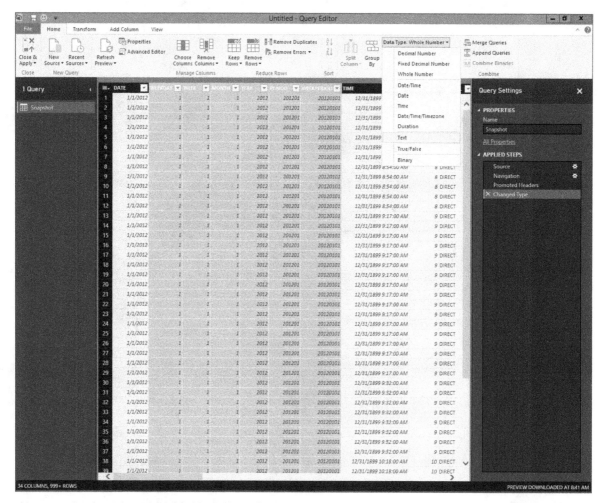

In this example, there are a lot of fields that are showing up as numerical fields when in fact they should be treated as text. Numerical fields are usually summed up by Power BI whereas Text fields are more dimensional. So in this example we select all of the fields that are numbers and then click on the **Data Type** dropdown list and mark them as **Text**.

Changing data's Data Types through the Query Editor

How to do it...

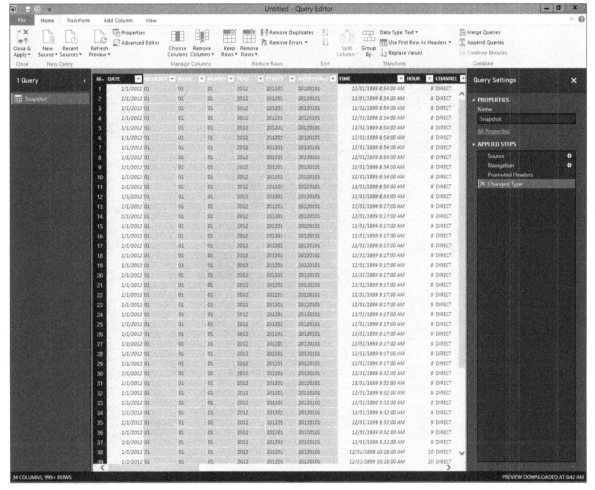

Now you will notice that all of the fields are showing up as text – the telltale sign is that they are all left justified.

www.dynamicscompanions.com
Dynamics Companions

- 53 -

www.blindsquirrelpublishing.com
© 2016 Blind Squirrel Publishing, LLC , All Rights Reserved

BLIND SQUIRREL
PUBLISHING

Changing data's Data Types through the Query Editor

How to do it...

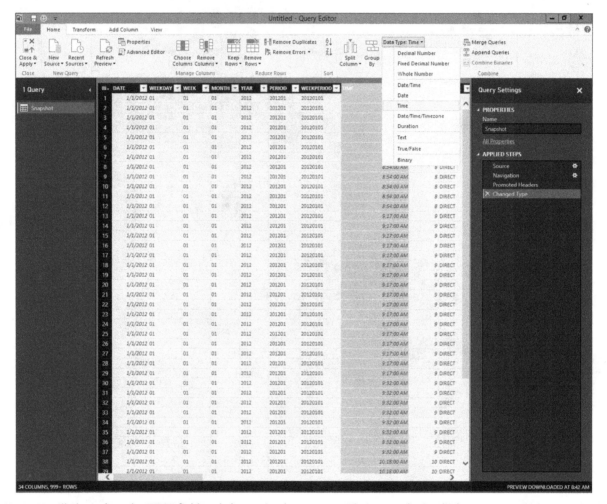

Next we will also select the **TIME** field and change its data type to **Time** to make it a little more concise.

Changing data's Data Types through the Query Editor

How to do it...

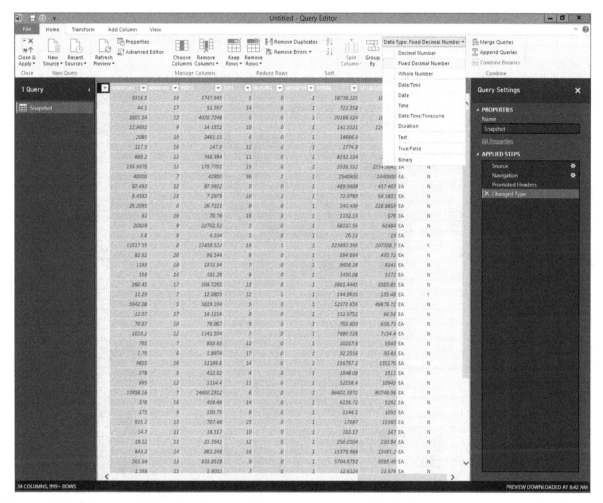

If we scroll further over into the data then we will also see a number of fields that are currency based. To tidy up the data we will change their data type to **Fixed Decimal Number** to get them ready to be marked as currency.

www.dynamicscompanions.com
Dynamics Companions

- 55 -

www.blindsquirrelpublishing.com
© 2016 Blind Squirrel Publishing, LLC, All Rights Reserved

BLIND SQUIRREL
PUBLISHING

Changing data's Data Types through the Query Editor

How to do it...

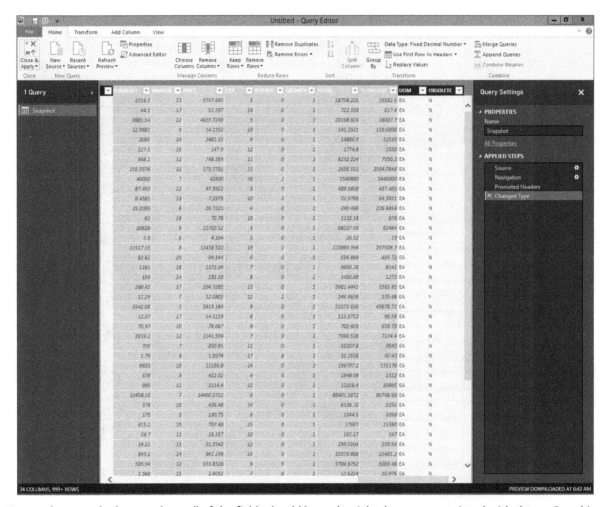

Now we have made these updates all of the fields should have the right datatype associated with them. One thing to point out at this point is that the Query Editor is tracking all of these changes for us and if you look over in the **Applied Steps** section of the Query Editor then you will see that there is a new step there called **Changed Type** which is storing all of these changes.

Changing data's Data Types through the Query Editor

How to do it...

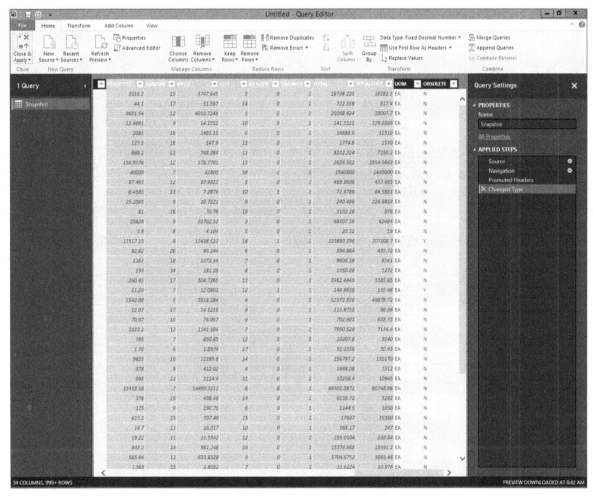

Now that we have made the changes to the query we can just click on the **Close & Apply** button to save the changes and return back to the main page of the designer.

www.dynamicscompanions.com
Dynamics Companions

- 57 -

www.blindsquirrelpublishing.com
© 2016 Blind Squirrel Publishing, LLC , All Rights Reserved

BLIND SQUIRREL
PUBLISHING

Accessing the Data Editor

Power BI Desktop is really a number of tools in one. So far we have seen the dashboard designer and the query editor, but if you really want to polish up the data and make it look more friendly to the user then you will want to look at the **Data Editor**.

How to do it...

To switch to the **Data Editor** view all you need to do is click on the icon on the left hand side of the application.

Accessing the Data Editor

How to do it...

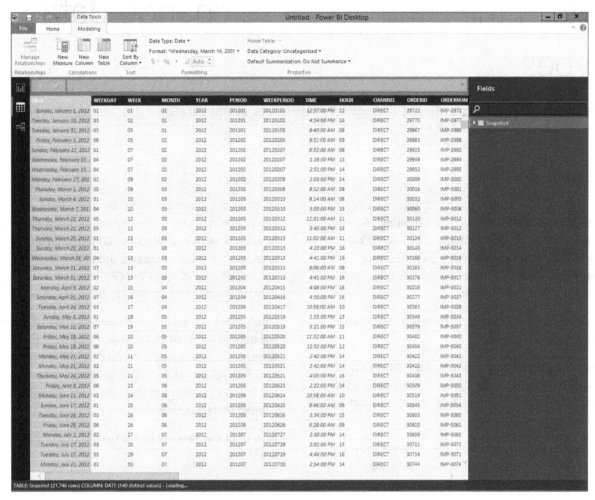

To switch to the **Data Editor** view all you need to do is click on the icon on the left hand side of the application.

Using the Data Editor to change data types

Through the Query Editor we changed some of the field data types, but the Data Editor gives us a number of other ways that we can format the data types.

How to do it...

To start off if we look at the **DATE** field, there is a little too much information that is showing. All we really want is the simple date. So if we select the **DATE** column we can then click on the **Format** dropdown, select the **Date Time** option and then choose a short date format.

Now you will see that the **DATE** data is formatted in the more concise way.

We can also change the format of the **TIME** field as well, and make it military time. This will allow us to graph the time more accurately without any sorting errors.

As you scroll through the data in the snapshot you will notice that there are a number of location specific fields there including the **CITY**, **STATE** etc. Power BI allows you to identify certain fields by their location type. If you select the **CITY** column and then select the **Data Category** dropdown list, then you will be able to select the **City** Data Category. You can do the same for **STATE**, **ZIP**, and **COUNTRY**.

Finally there are a number of currency based fields in the dataset like **STDCOST** that you may want to format as currency fields. To do that just select the column, click on the **Format** dropdown list, select the **Currency** option and then select the **$ English (United States)** option.

Now all of the data will be formatted just how we like it.

Using the Data Editor to change data types

How to do it...

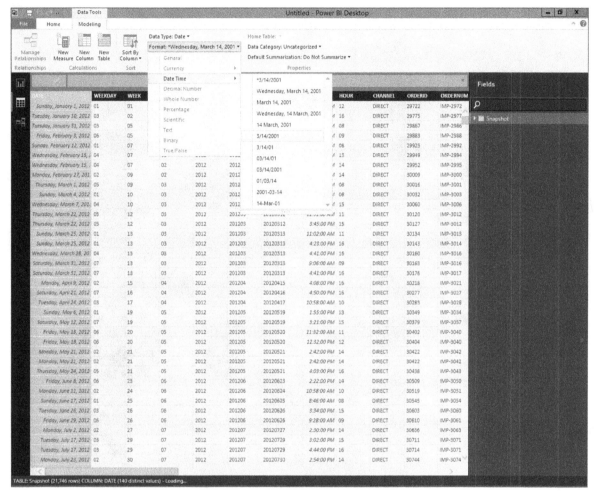

To start off if we look at the **DATE** field, there is a little too much information that is showing. All we really want is the simple date. So if we select the **DATE** column we can then click on the **Format** dropdown, select the **Date Time** option and then choose a short date format.

www.dynamicscompanions.com
Dynamics Companions

- 61 -

www.blindsquirrelpublishing.com
© 2016 Blind Squirrel Publishing, LLC , All Rights Reserved

BLIND SQUIRREL
PUBLISHING

Using the Data Editor to change data types

How to do it...

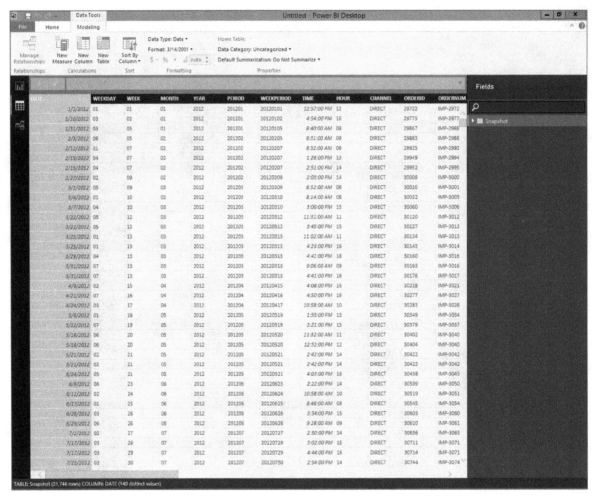

Now you will see that the **DATE** data is formatted in the more concise way.

www.dynamicscompanions.com
Dynamics Companions

www.blindsquirrelpublishing.com
© 2016 Blind Squirrel Publishing, LLC, All Rights Reserved

Using the Data Editor to change data types

How to do it...

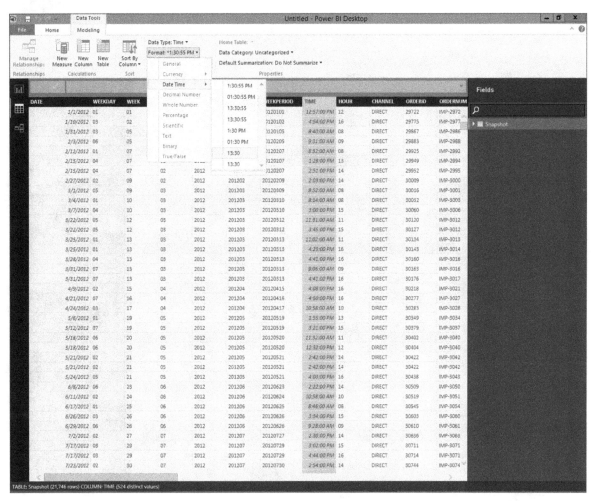

We can also change the format of the **TIME** field as well, and make it military time. This will allow us to graph the time more accurately without any sorting errors.

Using the Data Editor to change data types

How to do it...

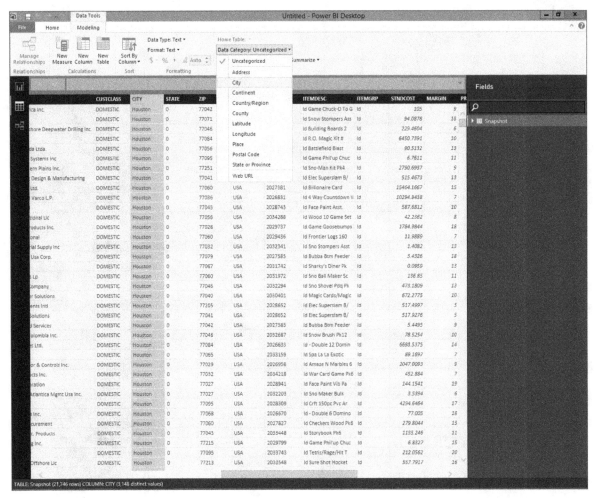

As you scroll through the data in the snapshot you will notice that there are a number of location specific fields there including the **CITY**, **STATE** etc. Power BI allows you to identify certain fields by their location type. If you select the **CITY** column and then select the **Data Category** dropdown list, then you will be able to select the **City** Data Category. You can do the same for **STATE**, **ZIP**, and **COUNTRY**.

Using the Data Editor to change data types

How to do it...

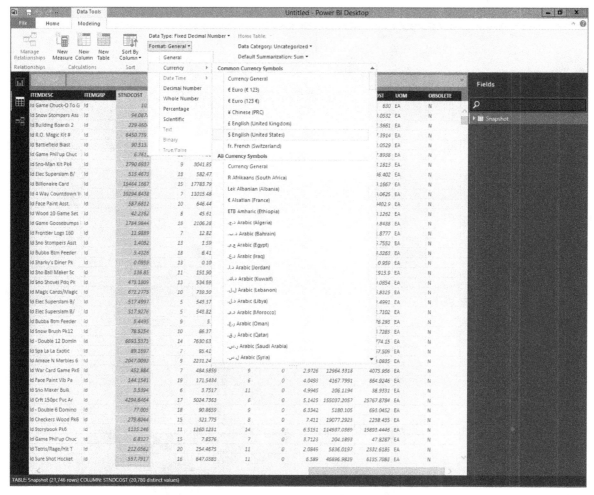

Finally there are a number of currency based fields in the dataset like **STDCOST** that you may want to format as currency fields. To do that just select the column, click on the **Format** dropdown list, select the **Currency** option and then select the **$ English (United States)** option.

dync

www.dynamicscompanions.com
Dynamics Companions

- 65 -

www.blindsquirrelpublishing.com
© 2016 Blind Squirrel Publishing, LLC , All Rights Reserved

BLIND SQUIRREL
PUBLISHING

Using the Data Editor to change data types

How to do it...

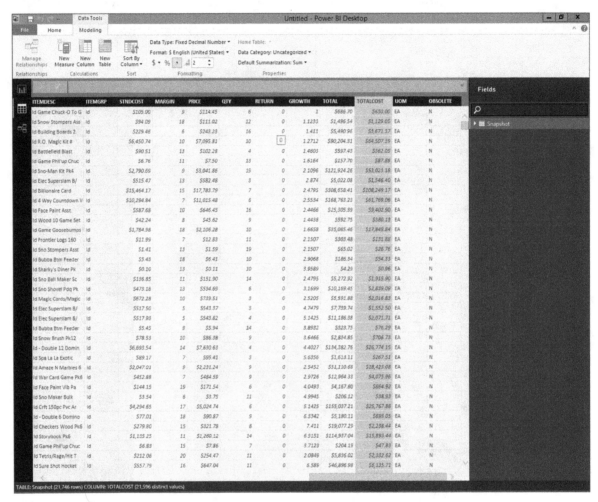

Now all of the data will be formatted just how we like it.

www.dynamicscompanions.com
Dynamics Companions

- 66 -

www.blindsquirrelpublishing.com
© 2016 Blind Squirrel Publishing, LLC, All Rights Reserved

BLIND SQUIRREL
PUBLISHING

Saving the Dashboard Projects

Now that we have made a few changes to the data, we may want to save the project away.

How to do it...

To save the project just click on the **Save** icon in the top left corner of the application, and when the **Save** dialog is displayed, give the project a file name and then click on the **Save** button.

www.dynamicscompanions.com
Dynamics Companions

- 67 -

www.blindsquirrelpublishing.com
© 2016 Blind Squirrel Publishing, LLC, All Rights Reserved

BLIND SQUIRREL
PUBLISHING

Saving the Dashboard Projects

How to do it...

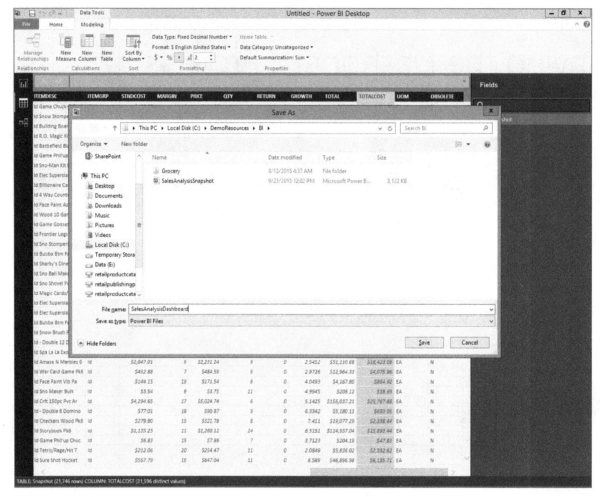

To save the project just click on the **Save** icon in the top left corner of the application, and when the **Save** dialog is displayed, give the project a file name and then click on the **Save** button.

Renaming fields to make them more friendly to the user

There is one last thing that we may want to do with our data before exiting from the **Data Editor** and that is to change the headings of the fields so that they are easier to read and also maybe a little more descriptive

How to do it...

To change the heading all you need to do is click on the column heading and then change the name. For example, click on the **DATE** column and rename it to **Date**. Not a huge change but it does look tidier.

Now repeat that for all of the other columns and you are done.

Renaming fields to make them more friendly to the user

How to do it...

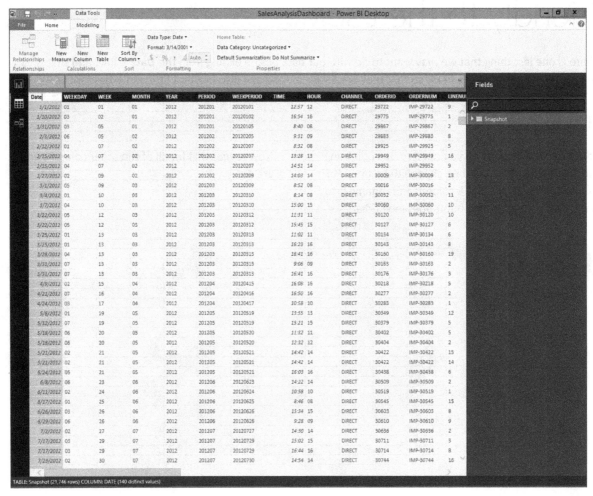

To change the heading all you need to do is click on the column heading and then change the name. For example, click on the **DATE** column and rename it to **Date**. Not a huge change but it does look tidier.

Renaming fields to make them more friendly to the user

How to do it...

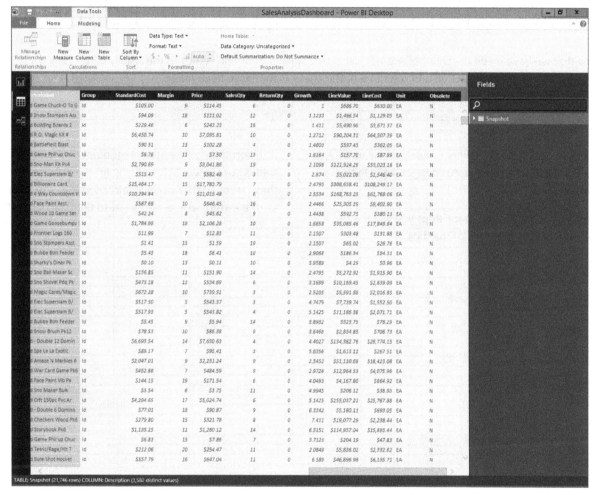

Now repeat that for all of the other columns and you are done.

www.dynamicscompanions.com
Dynamics Companions

- 71 -

www.blindsquirrelpublishing.com
© 2016 Blind Squirrel Publishing, LLC, All Rights Reserved

BLIND SQUIRREL
PUBLISHING

Viewing the changes in Query Editor

Now that we have made the changes, we will just take a small detour and return to the **Query Editor** that we accessed in the previous section and see some of the changes that have been made.

How to do it...

When you open up the **Query Editor** you will now see that there are some more changes listed in the **Applied Steps**.

If you click on any of the prior steps you will see the data as it was at that time of the data

transformation. The important point of this is that it shows how Power BI is building up the data from these steps so that when it refreshed the data then all of the steps are re-ran to get to the final data set.

Viewing the changes in Query Editor

How to do it...

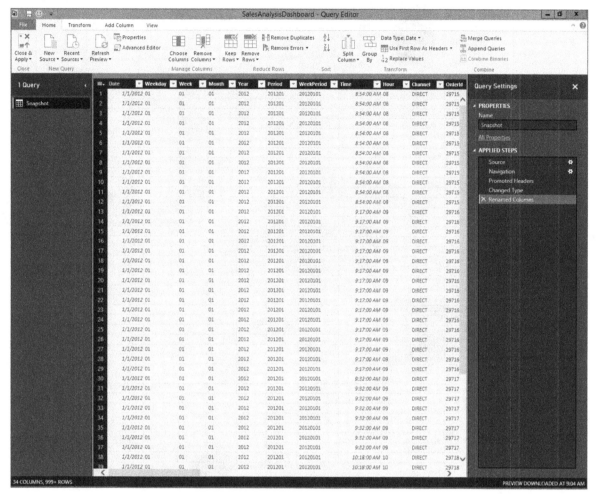

When you open up the **Query Editor** you will now see that there are some more changes listed in the **Applied Steps**.

Viewing the changes in Query Editor

How to do it...

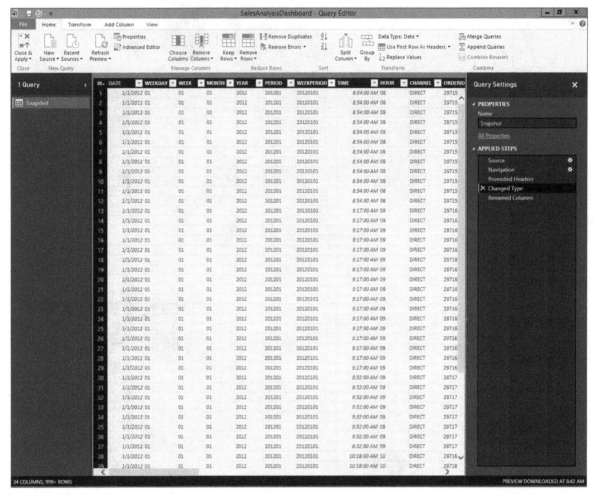

If you click on any of the prior steps you will see the data as it was at that time of the data transformation. The important point of this is that it shows how Power BI is building up the data from these steps so that when it refreshed the data then all of the steps are re-ran to get to the final data set.

Create more detailed dashboards

Now that we have massaged the data a little more we can try to build some more dashboards.

How to do it...

Click on the **Dashboard** icon on the left hand side to return to our initial dashboard that we created and you will see that it is still there even though we made changes to the data. What will look different will be all of the fields that are shown in the **Field Explorer** – they now look simpler.

To create new dashboards all you need to do is click on the fields again and ass them to the canvas.

www.dynamicscompanions.com
Dynamics Companions

- 75 -

www.blindsquirrelpublishing.com
© 2016 Blind Squirrel Publishing, LLC , All Rights Reserved

BLIND SQUIRREL
PUBLISHING

Create more detailed dashboards

How to do it...

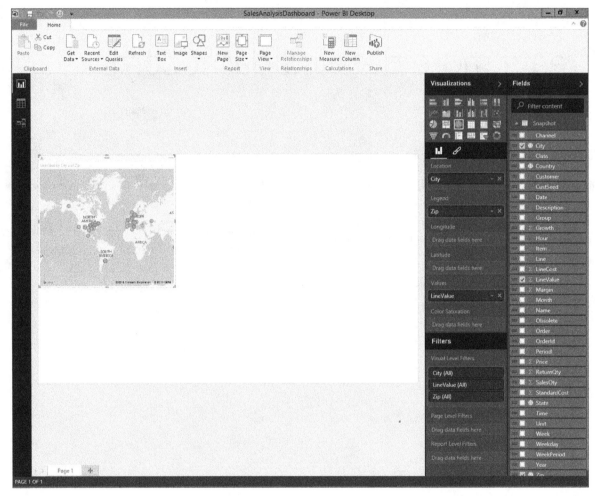

Click on the **Dashboard** icon on the left hand side to return to our initial dashboard that we created and you will see that it is still there even though we made changes to the data. What will look different will be all of the fields that are shown in the **Field Explorer** – they now look simpler.

Create more detailed dashboards

How to do it...

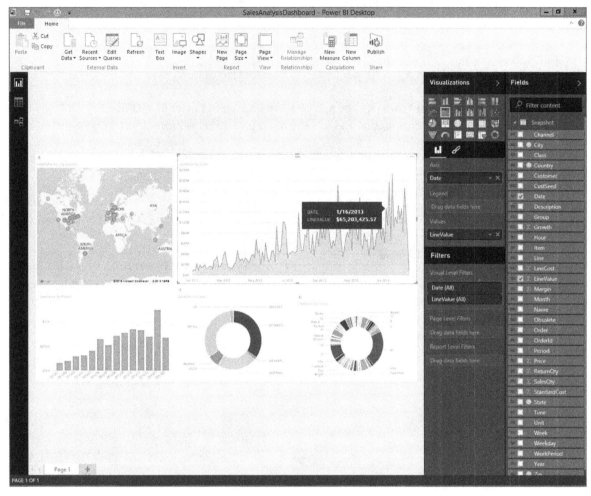

To create new dashboards all you need to do is click on the fields again and ass them to the canvas.

Publishing Dashboards to Power BI on Office365

Now that we have created our dashboards we can publish them back up to **Power BI** in **Office 365**. This will make them available to everyone in the organization and will also allow is to do some more clever things with the data.

How to do it...

To publish the Dashboard that we just created to **Office 365** just click on the **Publish** button within the **Share** group of the **Home** ribbon bar, and when the confirmation dialog is displayed, click **Save**.

The Desktop app will then connect to your **Office 365** account and publish the data up for you.

When everything is completed, you will get a cheery notice and then you can close out of the **Publishing** wizard.

When you return to **Power BI** on **Office 365** then you will see that there is now a **Report** that looks exactly the same as the dashboard that you just designed.

Publishing Dashboards to Power BI on Office365

How to do it...

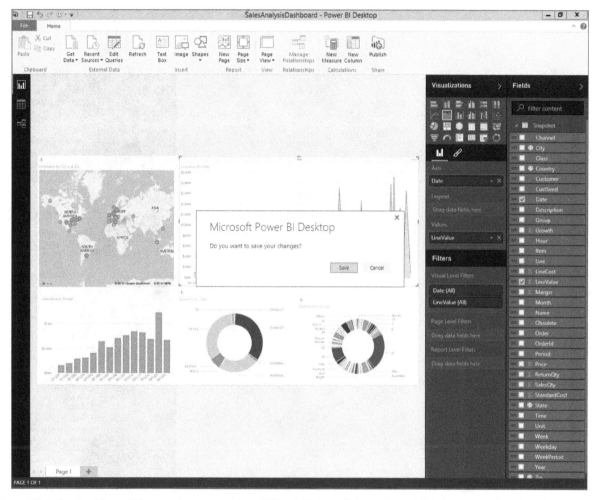

To publish the Dashboard that we just created to **Office 365** just click on the **Publish** button within the **Share** group of the **Home** ribbon bar, and when the confirmation dialog is displayed, click **Save**.

Publishing Dashboards to Power BI on Office365

How to do it...

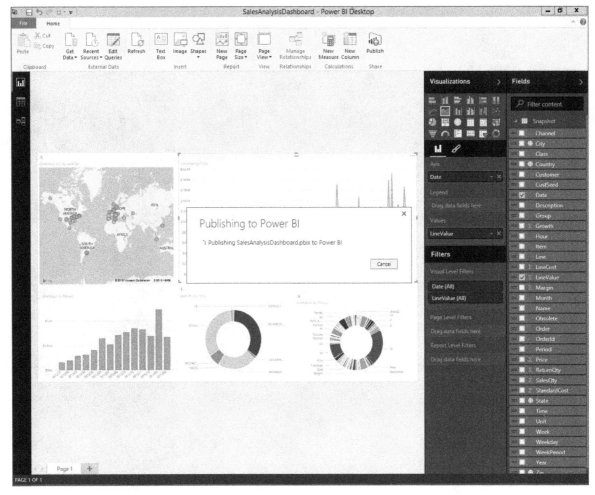

The Desktop app will then connect to your **Office 365** account and publish the data up for you.

Publishing Dashboards to Power BI on Office365

How to do it...

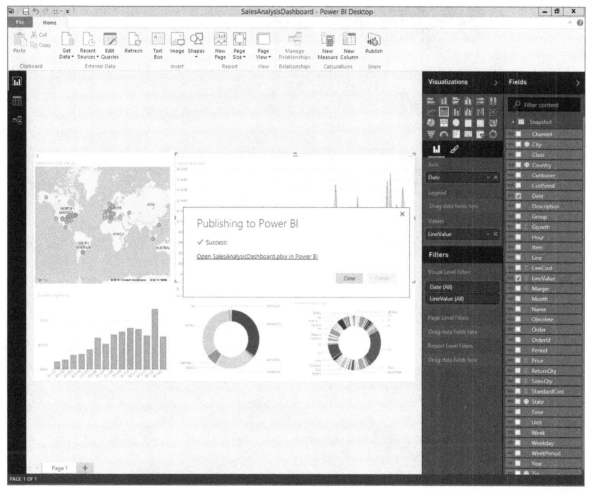

When everything is completed, you will get a cheery notice and then you can close out of the **Publishing** wizard.

dync

www.dynamicscompanions.com
Dynamics Companions

- 81 -

www.blindsquirrelpublishing.com
© 2016 Blind Squirrel Publishing, LLC , All Rights Reserved

BLIND SQUIRREL
PUBLISHING

Publishing Dashboards to Power BI on Office365

How to do it...

When you return to **Power BI** on **Office 365** then you will see that there is now a **Report** that looks exactly the same as the dashboard that you just designed.

Creating a new dashboard in Power BI Online

Power BI Online has one more additional feature that you can take advantage of and that is a concept of a **Dashboard**. Dashboards allow you to mash up data from multiple reports into one location that the user is then able to drill into, giving them one consolidated view.

How to do it...

To create a new dashboard, just click on the + button beside the **Dashboards** group within Power BI.

Then type in name of the dashboard – for example **Contoso Sales Summary**.

And you will be taken to a blank **Dashboard** canvas.

www.dynamicscompanions.com
Dynamics Companions

- 83 -

www.blindsquirrelpublishing.com
© 2016 Blind Squirrel Publishing, LLC , All Rights Reserved

BLIND SQUIRREL
PUBLISHING

Creating a new dashboard in Power BI Online

How to do it...

To create a new dashboard, just click on the **+** button beside the **Dashboards** group within Power BI.

Creating a new dashboard in Power BI Online

How to do it...

Then type in name of the dashboard – for example **Contoso Sales Summary**.

www.dynamicscompanions.com
Dynamics Companions

- 85 -

www.blindsquirrelpublishing.com
© 2016 Blind Squirrel Publishing, LLC , All Rights Reserved

BLIND SQUIRREL
PUBLISHING

Creating a new dashboard in Power BI Online

How to do it...

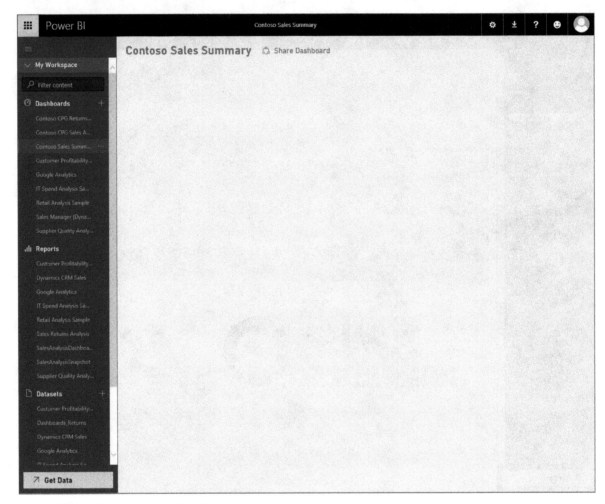

And you will be taken to a blank **Dashboard** canvas.

Pinning Report Tiles to your Dashboards

Now that we have a **Dashboard** we can start populating it with data from our report. To do this we just find the report chart that we want and the pin it.

How to do it...

So if you return back to the **SalesAnalysisDashboard** that was just imported, hover over any of the chart and you will notice that a pin shows up in the top right hand corner. All you need to do in order to add it to the dashboard is click on it.

This will open up a dialog box asking you which **Dashboard** you want to pin it to and all you need to do is click on the **Pin** button.

Power BI will tell you that the chart is now pinned to the Dashboard.

If you don't believe it then just click on the new **Dashboard** that you created and you will see it there.

Pinning Report Tiles to your Dashboards

How to do it...

So if you return back to the **SalesAnalysisDashboard** that was just imported, hover over any of the chart and you will notice that a pin shows up in the top right hand corner. All you need to do in order to add it to the dashboard is click on it.

Pinning Report Tiles to your Dashboards

How to do it...

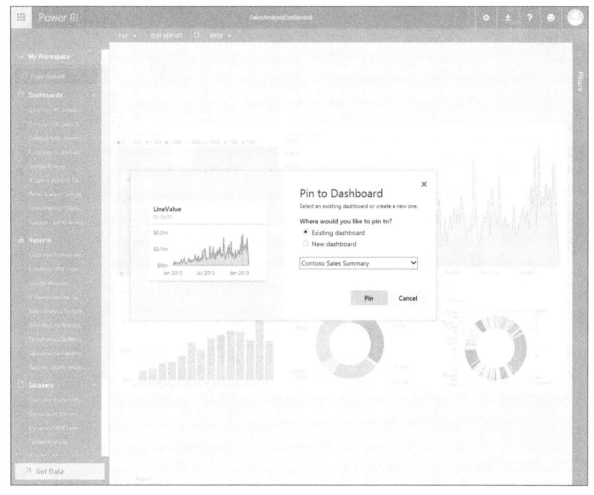

This will open up a dialog box asking you which **Dashboard** you want to pin it to and all you need to do is click on the **Pin** button.

Pinning Report Tiles to your Dashboards

How to do it...

Power BI will tell you that the chart is now pinned to the Dashboard.

Pinning Report Tiles to your Dashboards

How to do it...

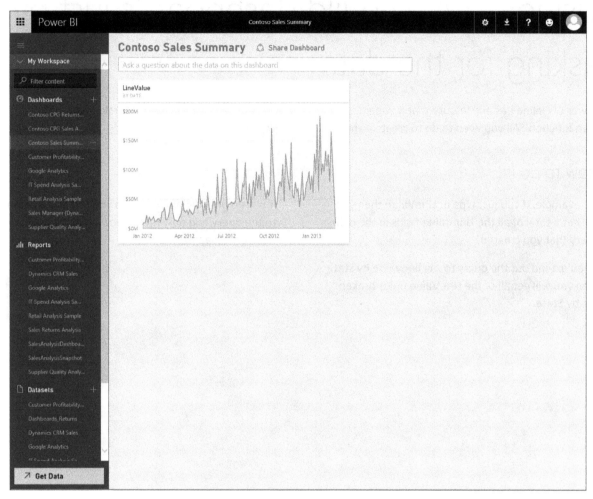

If you don't believe it then just click on the new **Dashboard** that you created and you will see it there.

Using Q&A to build dashboards just by asking for the data

Power BI Online has one feature that is super cool and is not available within the Desktop version and that is the Q&A function. All you need to do to create a chart or query is to ask Power BI as a question.

How to do it...

For example, if you just type in **LineValue** then you will get a total of all the **LineValue** fields in the data query that you created.

If you extend out the query to say **linevalue by state** then you will get all of the **LineValue** fields broken out by **State.**

If you go one step further then you can add **as map** to the query and now it will show all of the sales by state on a map for you.

Using Q&A to build dashboards just by asking for the data

How to do it...

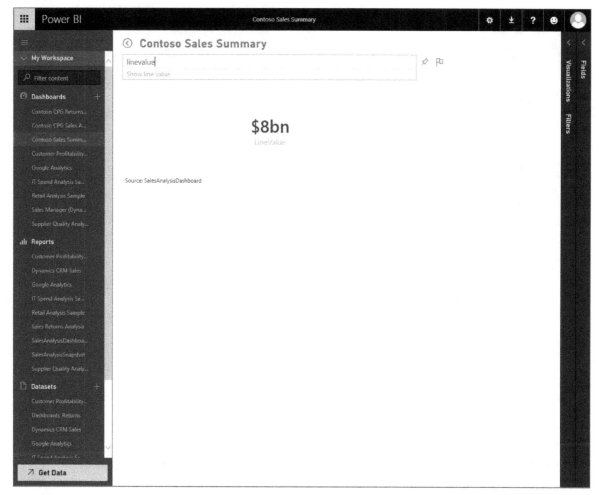

For example, if you just type in **LineValue** then you will get a total of all the **LineValue** fields in the data query that you created.

www.dynamicscompanions.com
Dynamics Companions

- 93 -

www.blindsquirrelpublishing.com
© 2016 Blind Squirrel Publishing, LLC , All Rights Reserved

BLIND SQUIRREL
PUBLISHING

Using Q&A to build dashboards just by asking for the data

How to do it...

If you extend out the query to say **linevalue by state** then you will get all of the **LineValue** fields broken out by **State.**

Using Q&A to build dashboards just by asking for the data

How to do it...

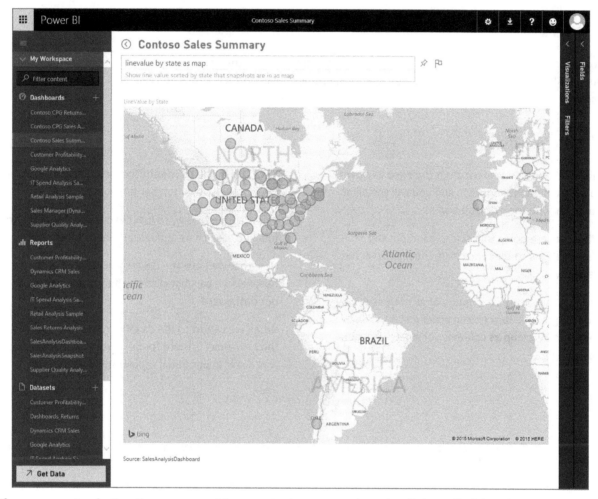

If you go one step further then you can add **as map** to the query and now it will show all of the sales by state on a map for you.

Using the Field Explorer to help find data

You can get even more elaborate with your queries by using more of the fields that you have defined in your query. All you need to know is what they are. To help you though there is a trick and that is to display the **Field Explorer**.

How to do it...

All you need to do is expand out the **Field Explorer** panel on the right hand side and you will see all of the fields with their default names.

While you are doing that also expand out the **Visualizations** so that you can manually tweak the views if you like.

Now we can create a summary of all of the sales by product group in descending order just by asking **linevalue by group as columns sorted by linevalue descending**.

If we add in the **by month** then we also get all of the sales broken down further by month.

This is a little messy, so just change the visualization to a line area chart and it looks much nicer.

Now that we have the Q&A chart created and tweaked we can just click on the pin and add it to our dashboard.

When we return to the dashboard we will now see the new chart is there for us to view even though it was never in our initial report that we created.

Using the Field Explorer to help find data

How to do it...

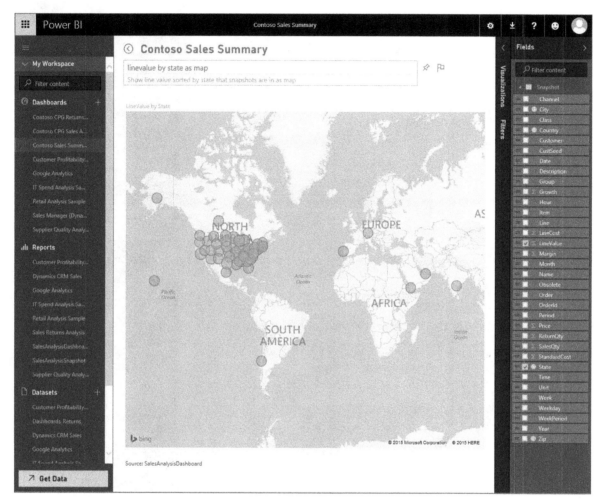

All you need to do is expand out the **Field Explorer** panel on the right hand side and you will see all of the fields with their default names.

dync
www.dynamicscompanions.com
Dynamics Companions
- 97 -
www.blindsquirrelpublishing.com
© 2016 Blind Squirrel Publishing, LLC , All Rights Reserved
BLIND SQUIRREL PUBLISHING

Using the Field Explorer to help find data

How to do it...

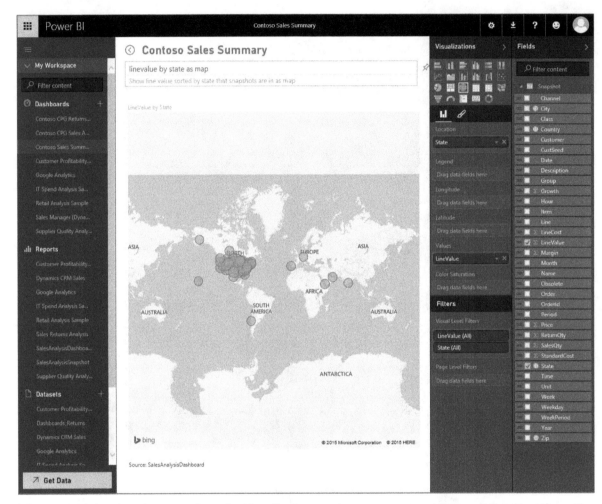

While you are doing that also expand out the **Visualizations** so that you can manually tweak the views if you like.

Using the Field Explorer to help find data

How to do it...

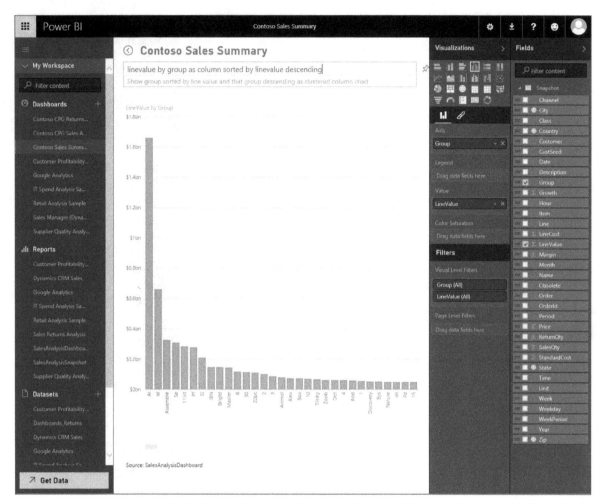

Now we can create a summary of all of the sales by product group in descending order just by asking **linevalue by group as columns sorted by linevalue descending**.

www.dynamicscompanions.com
Dynamics Companions

- 99 -

www.blindsquirrelpublishing.com
© 2016 Blind Squirrel Publishing, LLC , All Rights Reserved

BLIND SQUIRREL
PUBLISHING

Using the Field Explorer to help find data

How to do it...

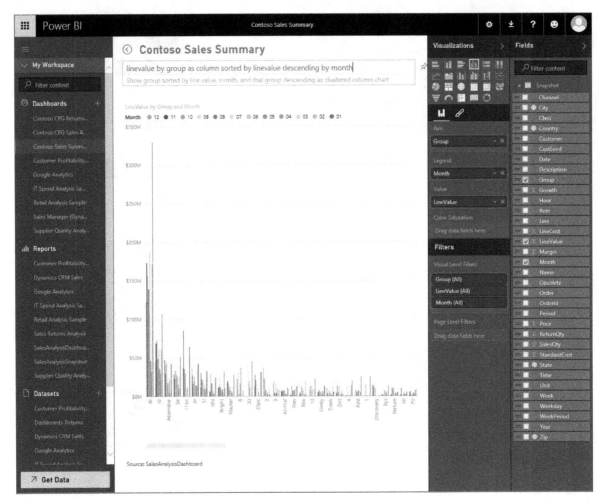

If we add in the **by month** then we also get all of the sales broken down further by month.

www.dynamicscompanions.com
Dynamics Companions

- 100 -

www.blindsquirrelpublishing.com
© 2016 Blind Squirrel Publishing, LLC , All Rights Reserved

BLIND SQUIRREL
PUBLISHING

Using the Field Explorer to help find data

How to do it...

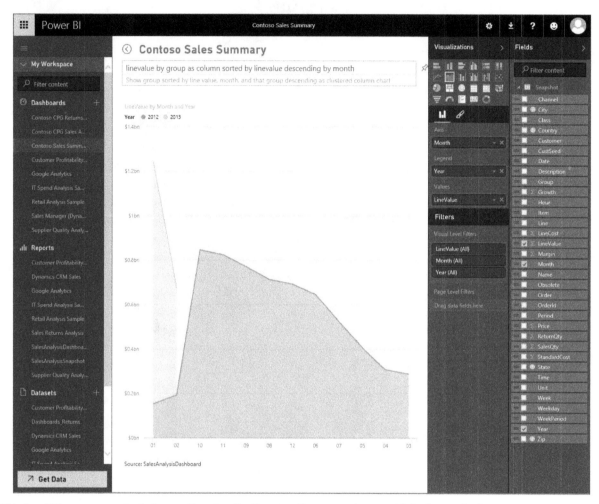

This is a little messy, so just change the visualization to a line area chart and it looks much nicer.

www.dynamicscompanions.com
Dynamics Companions

- 101 -

www.blindsquirrelpublishing.com
© 2016 Blind Squirrel Publishing, LLC, All Rights Reserved

BLIND SQUIRREL PUBLISHING

Using the Field Explorer to help find data

How to do it...

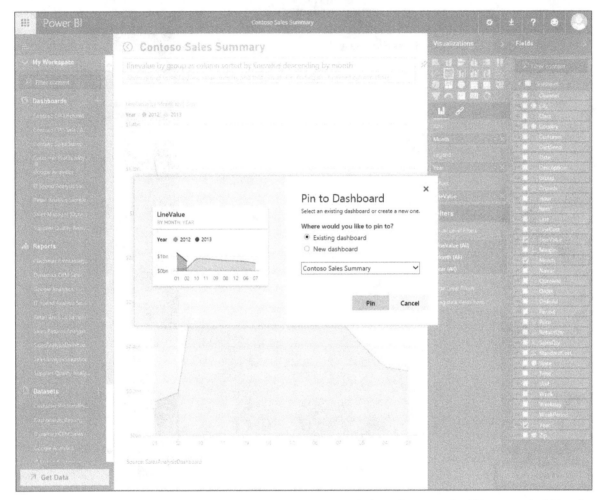

Now that we have the Q&A chart created and tweaked we can just click on the pin and add it to our dashboard.

www.dynamicscompanions.com
Dynamics Companions

- 102 -

www.blindsquirrelpublishing.com
© 2016 Blind Squirrel Publishing, LLC , All Rights Reserved

BLIND SQUIRREL
PUBLISHING

Using the Field Explorer to help find data

How to do it...

When we return to the dashboard we will now see the new chart is there for us to view even though it was never in our initial report that we created.

Downloading the Power BI Mobile App

You may think that this is more than enough BI options but there is one more way that we will look at our dashboards and that is through the free mobile app.

How to do it...

To get the Mobile App, all you need to do is click on the **Download** icon in the header of the **Power BI Online** workspace and click on the **Power BI Mobile** button.

This will take you to an invitation page where you will be asked have the link e-mailed to you.

If you click on it then it will send the link to you and you can just download the app from there.

Alternatively if you just go to any of the app stores and do a search on **Power BI** then you will find the app there and you can just install it.

www.dynamicscompanions.com
Dynamics Companions

- 104 -

Downloading the Power BI Mobile App

How to do it...

To get the Mobile App, all you need to do is click on the **Download** icon in the header of the **Power BI Online** workspace and click on the **Power BI Mobile** button.

Downloading the Power BI Mobile App

How to do it...

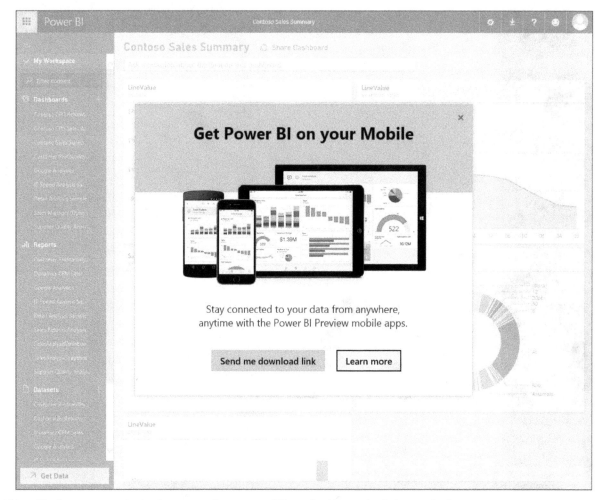

This will take you to an invitation page where you will be asked have the link e-mailed to you.

dync
www.dynamicscompanions.com
Dynamics Companions

- 106 -

www.blindsquirrelpublishing.com
© 2016 Blind Squirrel Publishing, LLC , All Rights Reserved

BLIND SQUIRREL
PUBLISHING

Downloading the Power BI Mobile App

How to do it...

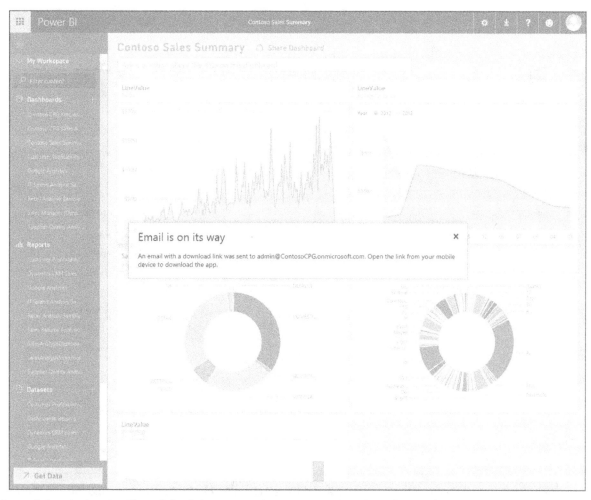

If you click on it then it will send the link to you and you can just download the app from there.

www.dynamicscompanions.com
Dynamics Companions
- 107 -
www.blindsquirrelpublishing.com
© 2016 Blind Squirrel Publishing, LLC , All Rights Reserved
BLIND SQUIRREL
PUBLISHING

Downloading the Power BI Mobile App

How to do it...

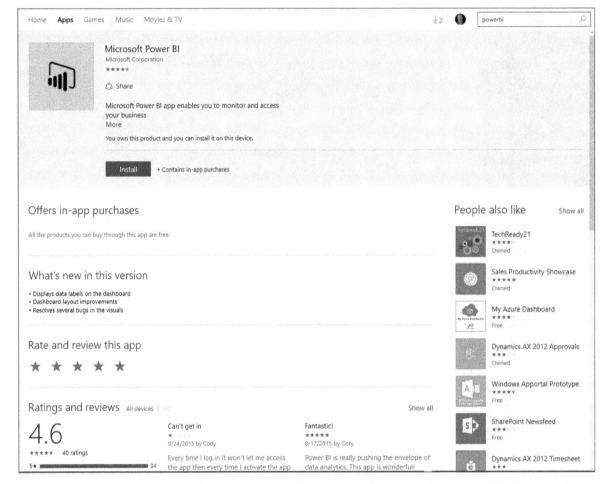

Alternatively if you just go to any of the app stores and do a search on **Power BI** then you will find the app there and you can just install it.

www.dynamicscompanions.com
Dynamics Companions

- 108 -

www.blindsquirrelpublishing.com
© 2016 Blind Squirrel Publishing, LLC , All Rights Reserved

BLIND SQUIRREL
PUBLISHING

Connecting the Power BI Mobile App to Power BI Online

Once you have downloaded the Mobile App all you need to do is connect it up to your Power BI Online account and it will do all of the rest for you.

How to do it...

To connect the Mobile App up all you need to do is open it up and then click on the **Sign in** button.

This will open up a Connection dialog and you just need to enter in the credentials that you use to log into your **O365** account and click on the **Sign in** button.

The Power BI Mobile App will then connect up and gather all of the dashboards that you have hosted on the server and make them available to you. All you need to do is click the **Let's Get Stated** button.

You will notice that the dashboard that we just created is immediately available to us and we can click on it.

That will take us straight to the dashboard showing us all of the same data as we saw on-line.

And if we need more information then we can just drill into the report detail and also filter out the data.

Connecting the Power BI Mobile App to Power BI Online

How to do it...

To connect the Mobile App up all you need to do is open it up and then click on the **Sign in** button.

Connecting the Power BI Mobile App to Power BI Online

How to do it...

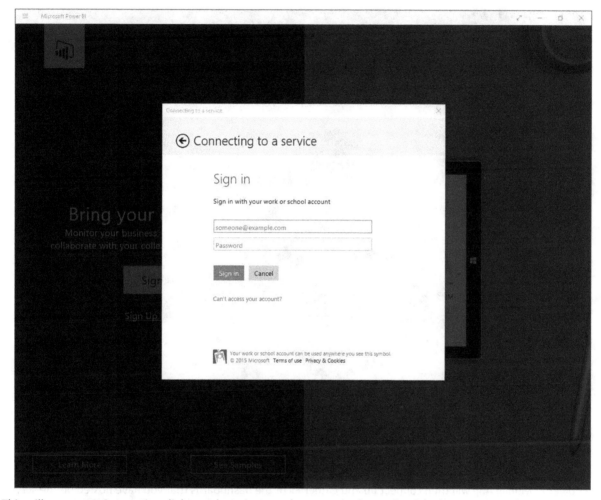

This will open up a Connection dialog and you just need to enter in the credentials that you use to log into your **O365** account and click on the **Sign in** button.

Connecting the Power BI Mobile App to Power BI Online

How to do it...

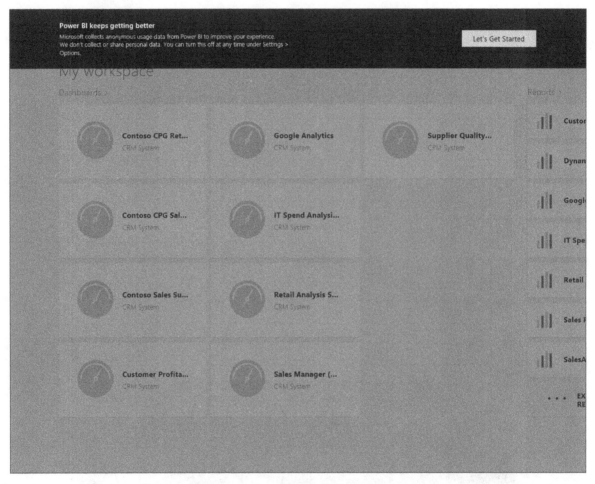

The Power BI Mobile App will then connect up and gather all of the dashboards that you have hosted on the server and make them available to you. All you need to do is click the **Let's Get Stated** button.

dync
www.dynamicscompanions.com
Dynamics Companions
- 112 -
www.blindsquirrelpublishing.com
© 2016 Blind Squirrel Publishing, LLC , All Rights Reserved
BLIND SQUIRREL
PUBLISHING

Connecting the Power BI Mobile App to Power BI Online

How to do it...

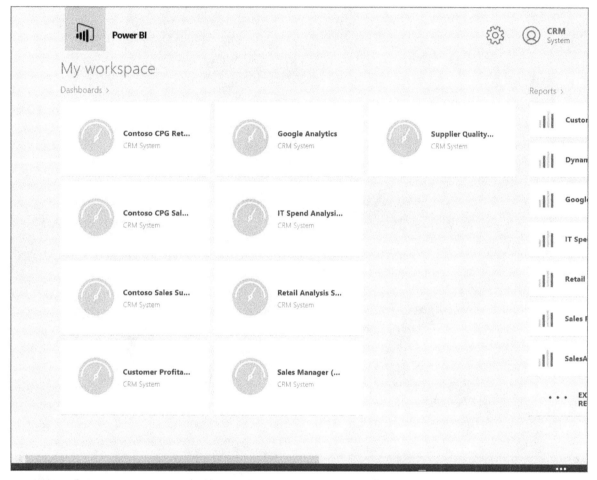

You will notice that the dashboard that we just created is immediately available to us and we can click on it.

Connecting the Power BI Mobile App to Power BI Online

How to do it...

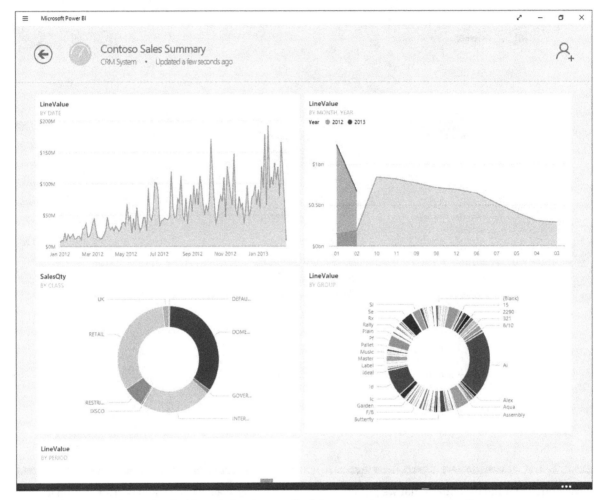

That will take us straight to the dashboard showing us all of the same data as we saw on-line.

Connecting the Power BI Mobile App to Power BI Online

How to do it...

And if we need more information then we can just drill into the report detail and also filter out the data.

Summary

In this presentation we have shown you how you can sign up for your very own Power BI hosted workspace, how you can download and use the **Desktop Designer** for free and create your own dashboards, and also how you can then publish those dashboards back up to Office 365 and Power BI online and further analyze the data. To make it even better all of this is then available through the Mobile application giving everyone access to your reports and dashboards even when they are on the go.

I think that this is enough excitement for this presentation, although make sure you all try this out. It is super cool and extremely useful to boot.

About The Author

Murray Fife is an Author of over 25 books on Microsoft Dynamics including the Bare Bones Configuration Guide series of over 15 books which step the user through the setup of initial Dynamics instance, then through the Financial modules and then through the configuration of the more specialized modules like production, service management, and project accounting. You can find all of his books on Amazon at www.amazon.com/author/murrayfife.

Murray is also the curator of the Dynamics Companions (www.dynamicscompanions.com) site which he built from the ground up as a resource for all of the Microsoft Dynamics community where you can find walkthroughs and blueprints that he created since first being introduced to the Microsoft Dynamics product.

For more information on Murray, here is his contact information:

Email: mcf@dynamicscompanions.com

Twitter: @murrayfife

Facebook: facebook.com/murraycfife

Google: google.com/+murrayfife

LinkedIn: linkedin.com/in/murrayfife

Blog: atinkerersnotebook.com

Docs: docs.com/mufife

Amazon: amazon.com/author/murrayfife

Need More Help with Dynamics AX 2012

The Bare Bones Configuration Guides for Microsoft Dynamics was developed to show you how to set up a company from the ground up and configure all of the common modules that most people would need, and a few that you might want to use.

It aims to demystify the setup process and prove that Dynamics is only as hard to configure as you make it, and if you are a mid-range customer that even you can get a company configured and working without turning on every bell and whistle and without breaking the bank.

There are 14 volumes in the current series and although each of these guides have been designed to stand by themselves as reference material for each of the modules within Dynamics, if they are taken as a whole series they are also a great training system that will allow even a novice on Dynamics AX work through the step by step instructions and build up a new company from scratch and learn a lot of the ins and outs of the system right away. The current guides are:

- Configuring a Training Environment
- Configuring The General Ledger
- Configuring Cash and Bank Management
- Configuring Accounts Receivable
- Configuring Accounts Payable
- Configuring Product Information Management
- Configuring Inventory Management
- Configuring Procurement & Sourcing
- Configuring Sales Order Management
- Configuring Human Resources
- Configuring Project Management & Accounting
- Configuring Production Control
- Configuring Sales & Marketing
- Configuring Service Management
-

If you are interested in finding out more about the series and also view all of the details including topics covered within the module, then browse to the Bare Bones Configuration Guide on the Dynamics Companions website. You will find all of the details, and also downloadable resources that help you with the setup of Microsoft Dynamics. Here is the full link:

http://www.dynamicscompanions.com

dyn c
www.dynamicscompanions.com
Dynamics Companions

- 119 -

www.blindsquirrelpublishing.com
© 2016 Blind Squirrel Publishing, LLC , All Rights Reserved

BLIND SQUIRREL
PUBLISHING

Usage Agreement

Blind Squirrel Publishing (the Owner) agrees to grant, and the user of the eBook agrees to accept, a nonexclusive license to use the eBook under the terms and conditions of this eBook License Agreement ("Agreement"). Your use of the eBook constitutes your agreement to the terms and conditions set forth in this Agreement. This Agreement, or any part thereof, cannot be changed, waived, or discharged other than by a statement in writing signed by you and Murray Fife. Please read the entire Agreement carefully.

EBook Usage. The eBook may be used by one user on any device. The user of the eBook shall be subject to all of the terms of this Agreement, whether or not the user was the purchaser.

Printing. You may occasionally print a few pages of the text (but not entire sections), which may include sending the printed pages to a third party in the normal course of your business, but you must warn the recipient in writing that copyright law prohibits the recipient from redistributing the eBook content to anyone else. Other than the above, you may not print pages and/or distribute eBook content to others.

Copyright, Use and Resale Prohibitions. The Author retains all rights not expressly granted to you in this Agreement. The software, content, and related documentation in the eBook are protected by copyright laws and international copyright treaties, as well as other intellectual property laws and treaties. Nothing in this Agreement constitutes a waiver of the author's rights. The Author will not be responsible for performance problems due to circumstances beyond its reasonable control. Other than as stated in this Agreement, you may not copy, print, modify, remove, delete, augment, add to, publish, transmit, sell, resell, license, create derivative works from, or in any way exploit any of the eBook's content, in whole or in part, in print or electronic form, and you may not aid or permit others to do so. The unauthorized use or distribution of copyrighted or other proprietary content is illegal and could subject the purchaser to substantial damages. Purchaser will be liable for any damage resulting from any violation of this Agreement.

No Transfer. This license is not transferable by the eBook purchaser unless such transfer is approved in advance by the Author.

Disclaimer. The eBook, or any support given by the Author are in no way substitutes for assistance from legal, tax, accounting, or other qualified professionals. If legal advice or other expert assistance is required, the services of a competent professional person should be sought.

Limitation of Liability. The eBook is provided "as is" and the Author does not make any warranty or representation, either express or implied, to the eBook, including its quality, accuracy, performance, merchantability, or fitness for a particular purpose. You assume the entire risk as to the results and performance of the eBook. The Author does not warrant, guarantee, or make any representations regarding the use of, or the results obtained with, the eBook in terms of accuracy, correctness or reliability. In no event will the Author be liable for indirect, special, incidental, or consequential damages arising out of delays, errors, omissions, inaccuracies, or the use or inability to use the eBook, or for interruption of the eBook, from whatever cause. This will apply even if the Author has been advised that the possibility of such damage exists. Specifically, the Author is not responsible for any costs, including those incurred as a result of lost profits or revenue, loss of data, the cost of recovering such programs or data, the cost of any substitute program, claims by third parties, or similar costs. Except for the Author's indemnification obligations in Section 7.2, in no case will the Author's liability exceed the amount of license fees paid.

Hold Harmless / Indemnification.
7.1 You agree to defend, indemnify and hold the Author and any third party provider harmless from and against all third party claims and damages (including reasonable attorneys' fees) regarding your use of the eBook, unless the claims or damages are due to the Author's or any third party provider's gross negligence or willful misconduct or arise out of an allegation for which the Author is obligated to indemnify you.
7.The Author shall defend, indemnify and hold you harmless at the Author's expense in any suit, claim or proceeding brought against you alleging that your use of the eBook delivered to you hereunder directly infringes a United States patent, copyright, trademark, trade secret, or other third party proprietary right, provided the Author is (i) promptly notified, (ii) given the assistance required at the Author's expense, and (iii) permitted to retain legal counsel of the Author's choice and to direct the defense. The Author also agrees to pay any damages and costs awarded against you by final judgment of a court of last resort in any such suit or any agreed settlement amount on account of any such alleged infringement, but the Author will have no liability for settlements or costs incurred without its consent. Should your use of any such eBook be enjoined, or in the event that the Author desires to minimize its liability hereunder, the Author will, at its option and expense, (i) substitute a fully equivalent non-infringing eBook for the infringing item; (ii) modify the infringing item so that it no longer infringes but remains substantially equivalent; or (iii) obtain for you the right to continue use of such item. If none of the foregoing is feasible, the Author will terminate your access to the eBook and refund to you the applicable fees paid by you for the infringing item(s). THE FOREGOING STATES THE ENTIRE LIABILITY OF THE AUTHOR AND YOUR SOLE REMEDY FOR INFRINGEMENT OR FOR ANY BREACH OF WARRANTY OF NON-INFRINGEMENT, EXPRESS OR IMPLIED. THIS INDEMNITY WILL NOT APPLY TO ANY ALLEGED INFRINGEMENT BASED UPON A COMBINATION OF OTHER SOFTWARE OR INFORMATION WITH THE EBOOK WHERE THE EBOOK WOULD NOT HAVE OTHERWISE INFRINGED ON ITS OWN.